Tactics for Racial Justice

This is not a book of antiracist theory but antiracist tactics – tactics that anyone, of any race, can use to strike a blow against injustice. Antiracism is not about what we feel but what we do, and there are specific techniques we can use to create a just world.

Antiracist strategies are skills that can be learned just as we learn skills for public speaking or hitting a baseball. In these pages, you – whether a person of color or white – will find a playbook for leading your workplace, organization, or community through transformative change in the wake of an act of explicit racism. You'll learn to play antiracist rhetorical chess, and to anticipate and effectively respond to the discursive moves of people who don't understand bigotry, aren't aware of it, are in denial of it, or even actively uphold it – so that you can advance justice goals. You'll get a blueprint of how to dismantle systemic racism community by community, workplace by workplace, and organization by organization – and examples of what not to do.

This book is aimed at people who are conscious of the reality of racism and want to end it but may not know how. It clearly shows how anyone can make an effective, significant, and measurable impact on racism through strategic action.

Shannon Joyce Prince earned her doctorate in African and African American Studies and her master's in English from Harvard University Graduate School of Arts and Sciences, her law degree from Yale Law School, and her bachelor's degree magna cum laude from Dartmouth College. She practices law at Boies Schiller Flexner.

Giving Voice to Values
Series Editor: Mary C. Gentile

The *Giving Voice to Values* series is a collection of books on Business Ethics and Corporate Social Responsibility that brings a practical, solutions-oriented, skill-building approach to the salient questions of values-driven leadership.

Giving Voice to Values (GVV: www.GivingVoiceToValues.org) – the curriculum, the pedagogy and the research upon which it is based – was designed to transform the foundational assumptions upon which the teaching of business ethics is based, and importantly, to equip future business leaders to know not only what is right – but how to make it happen.

Professionalism and Values in Law Practice
Robert Feldman

Giving Voice to Values in the Boardroom
Cynthia E. Clark

Giving Voice to Values
An Innovation and Impact Agenda
Jerry Goodstein and Mary C. Gentile

Collaborating for Climate Resilience
Ann Goodman and Nilda M. Mesa

Tactics for Racial Justice
Building an Antiracist Organization and Community
Shannon Joyce Prince

For more information about this series, please visit: www.routledge.com/Giving-Voice-to-Values/book-series/GVV

Tactics for Racial Justice

Building an Antiracist Organization and Community

Shannon Joyce Prince

LONDON AND NEW YORK

First published 2022
by Routledge
4 Park Square, Milton Park, Abingdon, Oxon OX14 4RN

and by Routledge
605 Third Avenue, New York, NY 10158

Routledge is an imprint of the Taylor & Francis Group, an informa business

© 2022 Shannon Joyce Prince

The right of Shannon Joyce Prince to be identified as author of this work has been asserted in accordance with sections 77 and 78 of the Copyright, Designs and Patents Act 1988.

All rights reserved. No part of this book may be reprinted or reproduced or utilised in any form or by any electronic, mechanical, or other means, now known or hereafter invented, including photocopying and recording, or in any information storage or retrieval system, without permission in writing from the publishers.

Trademark notice: Product or corporate names may be trademarks or registered trademarks, and are used only for identification and explanation without intent to infringe.

British Library Cataloguing-in-Publication Data
A catalogue record for this book is available from the British Library

Library of Congress Cataloging-in-Publication Data
A catalog record has been requested for this book

ISBN: 978-0-367-70026-3 (hbk)
ISBN: 978-0-367-70028-7 (pbk)
ISBN: 978-1-003-14429-8 (ebk)

DOI: 10.4324/9781003144298

Typeset in Bembo
by codeMantra

For my nephew Noah – this book is my attempt to help create a world worthy of you.

Contents

Foreword		ix
Acknowledgments		xiii
	Introduction – the antiracist journey: moving from feeling to fighting	1
1	eading in the wake of an act of explicit racism	5
2	Antiracism rhetorical chess: how to discuss and debate racism effectively	30
3	Unweaving systemic racism	51
4	Reckoning with the past	79
5	Making powerful change when you lack political, institutional, or… any power	109
	Epilogue – ancestors and avatars: becoming what the future requires	119
Index		123

Foreword

Shannon Prince's book appears at just the right time.

America – along with parts of the rest of the world – is in the midst of an extraordinary transformation. That transformation is long overdue, yet it is happening so fast that we may forget to appreciate just how much is changing. When I began work on my own book, *Learning from the Germans: Race and the Memory of Evil* in 2016, the idea that Americans needed to face their racist history as the Germans have (partly) faced theirs was considered highly provocative. Five years later, millions of Americans no longer find it controversial to acknowledge the depth of the racism in our country's past, nor its murderous consequences in the present. Perhaps the spectacle of an American president praising white supremacists carrying Nazi symbols as "very fine people" provoked a wave of nausea that made many conclude that *something* must be done. And many forces have contributed to this transformation through an array of books and films, magnificent achievements like the National Memorial for Peace and Justice, and the powerful efforts of Black Lives Matter.

To our everlasting shame, George Floyd's murder, as we may now legally call it, generated outrage among millions of Americans of all races, but that outrage did not prevent the police killings of over 1,000 people, disproportionately Black men. One thing this shows is that expressions of outrage, or guilt, are never enough to combat racism. So, what steps can those of us, whether white or non-white, take to move beyond outrage and guilt in order to work effectively toward ending racism?

Shannon Prince is perfectly placed to answer this question. She is a Black woman who has successfully navigated majority-white elite spaces – Dartmouth, Harvard, Yale Law School, and now a major law firm – while engaging in antiracist work since her first semester in college. Using examples from her own work as well as from history and the social sciences, she lays out clear, concrete, and practical steps that take us from wanting to do something or other to combat racism to becoming a useful antiracist. She argues that effective antiracism is not a mindset but a skillset, not a matter of feeling but an assortment of practices we can learn. Just like other skills, from dancing to playing a sport or an instrument, these practices need to be honed, repeated, and honed again before they can be done really well. As Prince writes, Martin Luther King may have had a dream, but you need a plan.

Prince provides us with detailed plans for increasing racial diversity, and justice, in our communities and workspaces. She shows us how to conduct antiracist conversations that do not trigger defensive backlash – in other words, conversations that actually work to change other people's minds and actions. She also shows us how to recognize unconscious bias with examples that go beyond those which have become familiar. Prince's approach is both moral and pragmatic, and she describes how we can use both angles to effect real change. She presents tactics in dialogues designed to recognize, and prevent, the sort of excuses with which antiracist attempts are often diverted. *If this doesn't work, try that. If you hear this polite dismissal, be more forceful by saying this.* She shows us how treating your colleague or employer respectfully and empathetically – even when she doesn't deserve it – yields far better results than a self-righteous harangue. She also shows how these tactics can be used whether you are white or non-white, whether you have power or stand low in your local hierarchy.

Shannon Prince is a universalist, and she practices what she preaches. She is committed to fighting injustice wherever it occurs, and has devoted much of her professional life to legal representation of Native American nations. Her writing is as clear as it is reasonable, and she is determined to avoid the pointless polemics and virtue-signaling that have marred recent bestsellers purporting to heal racial divides. Her book ends with an appeal to think of ourselves as ancestors: to live our lives with the gravity and intensity that comes from the knowledge that our actions will shape the world we leave behind us. Just as racism was shaped by the actions of generations of individuals whose deeds combined to create structures that still oppress and destroy lives, so each of us can have a hand in dismantling those structures.

For the first time in our history, Americans are reckoning with the centrality of slavery and its aftermath, for which the expression "Jim Crow" is a wholly inadequate euphemism for what Bryan Stevenson rightly calls the age of racial terror. Perhaps even more surprisingly, we are beginning to acknowledge the murder of Native American peoples and theft of Native American lands that lay at the very heart of the American project. We should not be discouraged by the backlash that such a reckoning inevitably provokes among those unwilling to acknowledge the depth and the force of white supremacy. Even in Germany, decades of hard work were needed before a majority of Germans were able to recognize the horror of Nazi crimes. So backlash in America should not dishearten us, but we do need to learn how to counter that backlash effectively. Prince offers a roadmap, and too much is at stake now to ignore it.

Prince's book takes us to the next step, beyond *How to Be an Antiracist* by Ibram X. Kendi and *White Fragility: Why It's So Hard for White People to Talk about Racism* by Robin Di Angelo, to share actual tactics for fixing the problems those books address. Read *Tactics for Racial Justice*, and give a copy to someone you know who is seeking leadership, good sense, and guidelines for real change.

— Susan Neiman
Berlin, May 2021

Acknowledgments

In 2016, I had the privilege of being a Fellow at Auschwitz for the Study of Professional Ethics in Law, an organization on whose Alumni Steering Committee I now serve. Though Friedrich Wilhelm Nietzsche warned that those who fight monsters risk becoming them, FASPE's philosophy is that those who study perpetrators of monstrous deeds can deepen their own commitment to and capacity for moral action.

But FASPE faculty member Professor Mary Gentile of University of Virginia Darden School of Business taught not about perpetrators but heroes – about scholarly research into the nature of Holocaust rescuers. What that research showed is that one reason Holocaust rescuers took on the role of hero is that they had trained for it. The Giving Voice to Values book series that Mary edits and of which this book is part is inspired by the research-informed idea that we *all* can train ourselves into heroism. Thank you so very much, Mary, for inviting me to contribute a book to your series. And deepest thanks to the entire FASPE community, especially Founder and Chairman David Goldman, Executive Director Thorsten Wagner, Development Manager Mia Garcia, and Program Director Rebecca Scott.

Mary was inspired to reach out to me about writing this book after watching a FASPE webinar *Learning from the Germans: Confronting the Legacy of Racism in the Professions* in which I had the honor of being a co-panelist with Dr. Susan Neiman, director of the Einstein Forum and author of *Learning from the Germans: Race and the Memory of Evil*. Susan, thank you for the example you have set of confronting the grotesque with grace.

Finally, thank you to my loved ones for being family I would choose as friends and friends who are as dear as family. I cherish your support.

Introduction – the antiracist journey
Moving from feeling to fighting

Maybe it was the expression on ex-Officer Chauvin's face as he knelt on George Floyd's neck, that smirk of someone savoring a sin; maybe it was the sound of George Floyd rasping, again and again, "I can't breathe," crying out to the ghost of his late mother as he, too, faded to phantom;[1] maybe it was recollecting that you'd heard those words before somewhere – oh yes, when a Black man named Eric Garner was choked to death by the police officer detaining him for selling loose cigarettes....[2] Maybe it's those words echoing down the corridor of your heart in the voice of Elijah McClain, the young, self-taught Black violinist who died after being choked by the police for... well, for no reason at all;[3] echoing in the voice of Manuel Ellis, the Black church musician beaten and deprived of oxygen by the police;[4] echoing in the voice of Derek Scott, another Black man killed by the police. ... He said, "I can't breathe." An officer replied, "I don't care."[5]

Maybe it was one of those moments that sent you to the internet, to the bookstore, or to an acquaintance of color to learn about racism which led you to discover that one in three Native American women will be raped in her lifetime, and approximately seventy percent of the perpetrators are white;[6] that Black American women with postgraduate degrees are more likely to bear babies that succumb to infant mortality than the babies of white women whose educations terminated in the eighth grade – or earlier;[7] that, all things being equal, white men with prison records receive more callbacks on their job applications than Black men without them because when you're looking for a job, being Black counts against you more than being an ex-con.[8] Or maybe you're one of the people of color who has suffered those atrocities. No matter your racial background, people of character who are conscious of the reality of racism want to end it yet may not know *how*. Once you've made the resolution to demolish oppression, you might wonder: "Now what?" What, exactly, are concrete steps *I* can take?

That's what this book is about.

Antiracism is not something one *feels* but a skillset one uses to *fight* prejudice. It's a praxis, not an ontological state. And it's a journey that requires us to have a growth mindset rather than a fixed mindset. As psychologist

DOI: 10.4324/9781003144298-1

Dr. Carol Dweck explains in her book *Mindset: The New Psychology of Success*, people with fixed mindsets believe that their talents and abilities are inborn and pretty much unalterable, while people with growth mindsets believe that who they are and what they can do are capable of being developed. Unsurprisingly, the latter are more successful than the former.

Unfortunately, we often have fixed mindsets about antiracism – *and* racism. We tell ourselves, "Antiracism is for 'activists' – not for regular people like me." "I'm too old to learn the new rules of political correctness and keep up with ever-changing mores – I'll leave that stuff to the younger generation." "I'd like to fight racism, but I'm afraid that if I tried, I'd only say the wrong thing." "One time, I attempted to stand up to racism, and things didn't go how I expected, so I don't think I'll try again." "I admit I *do* hold negative attitudes about X racial group, but I don't think I can change."

People with fixed mindsets believe that "antiracist" is either something you *are* or you *aren't* – like being left-handed. And if they feel that they *aren't*, they assume there's nothing they can do about it. *And*, too often, if they feel that they *are*, they take for granted that there's nothing they *need* do about it – they believe that *being* antiracist is sufficient; *acting* antiracist is not required. In contrast, when we think of antiracism as a practice, we employ a growth mindset. We realize that antiracism is like golf – we can pick it up at any age; that antiracists aren't a special type of people – they're regular people who have chosen to develop a special set of skills. We understand that we don't have to *be* experts on race, racism, and antiracism – we can *cultivate* expertise. And we also understand that simply *believing* that all people are equal is not enough – we must develop skills and strategies to ensure that they are treated as such.

Consider: if you're on a sports team, you don't expect to win the game by *feeling* like an athlete, by *understanding* that you should make baskets or run touchdowns, or by *hoping* to score points. You sketch out plays. You run drills. You attend practices. Similarly, if you're in the army and preparing to go to war against an enemy, you don't anticipate triumphing simply by yearning to be successful in battle, by affirming the justice of your cause, or by telling others that your opponents are wrong. You come up with a plan, you gather weaponry, and you act in concert with your troop. Or what about if you're a scientist trying to cure a disease? You don't sit idly around your laboratory having faith that future generations will figure out a remedy or fantasizing that the sickness will fade out slowly over the generations on its own or comforting yourself with the notion that at least the illness isn't as grievous as it was in previous eras. Yet somehow, many of us believe that if we're in a match – a war – against racial injustice, if we're trying to cure society of the sickness of bigotry, success can be achieved by holding the right attitudes... when what's required is taking the right *actions*.

We simply cannot afford to think otherwise. For example, Blacks and whites use and sell drugs at similar rates. (Black people use less than one percent more than whites; whites sell a few percentage points more than Blacks.)

But Blacks are 2.7 times more likely to be arrested for drug crimes.[9] And the police stop and search Black drivers based on less evidence suggestive of possible wrongdoing than they do white drivers – even though white drivers are more likely to have illegal items on them.[10]

What this situation shows is that bigotry transcends the realm of attitude to become *action*. Thus, stopping Black drivers from being searched more or Black people from being arrested more – or eradicating any other form of injustice – requires more than sentiment.... It requires strategy.

The good thing is antiracist strategies are skills that can be learned just as we learn skills for public speaking or hitting a baseball or cooking. Each chapter of *Tactics* offers stories and case examples to show how anyone can make an effective, significant, and measurable impact on racism through strategic action.

Because it is often spectacular acts of prejudice that shock us into participating in the fight against racism, Chapter 1 provides a blueprint for leading your community, workplace, or organization toward justice and healing in the wake of an explicit incident of bigotry. Chapter 2 teaches one of the most important skills for advancing justice goals: learning how to speak powerfully and *persuasively* to people who don't understand bigotry, aren't aware of it, are in denial of it, or even actively uphold it. And special attention is paid to *cross-racial* dialogue. Chapter 3 deals with the most common – and most powerful – form of racism: that which is institutional and systemic. The development of antiracist systems can change institutions into justice powerhouses, so this chapter provides a map for creating systems that transform your community, workplace, or organization.

From the curricula in our schools to the statues in our squares to the flags in our skies, we are constantly confronted with evidence that history is not past but perennial. Chapter 4 limns how to lead your community, workplace, or institution through the process of navigating fraught but crucial issues such as celebration, reparation, and other forms of reckoning, for unless the past is faced with moral courage, the present will remain dystopian.

Confronted with a problem as mammoth as racism, many believe that you can't make change if you aren't in charge. But even someone acting alone and without authority can strike a powerful blow against racism... *if* he or she acts strategically. Chapter 5 explains how to be a dynamic counter-racist force in your community, workplace, or organization even without institutional control – or support.

Finally, the Epilogue reminds us that a just future requires that we act like ancestors, that we go about our quotidian lives with gravity and intensity, and regard them with precocious retrospection. And it demands that, like avatars, we realize that our deeds and abstentions either create, sustain, or destroy the fabric of the moral universe. Racism was established by individuals, great and humble, who recognized that power within themselves. And it will only be destroyed by them.

By *you*.

Notes

1 The Associated Press, "Floyd Transcript: Read It in Full Here," *TwinCities. com Pioneer Press*, July 9, 2020, https://www.twincities.com/2020/07/09/george-floyd-transcript-read-it-in-full-here/.
2 "Eric Garner: No Federal Charges in US 'I Can't Breathe' Death," *BBC News*, July 17, 2019, https://www.bbc.com/news/world-us-canada-49008746.
3 Grant Stringer, "Unlikely Suspect: Those Who Knew Elijah Balk at Aurora Police Account of His Death," *Sentinel Colorado*, October 27, 2019, https://sentinelcolorado.com/news/metro/unlikely-suspect-those-who-knew-elijah-balk-at-aurora-police-account-of-his-death/; Kim Bellware, "Police Had No Legal Reason to Place Elijah McClain in Chokehold, Probe of Death Finds," *Washington Post*, February 23, 2021, https://www.washingtonpost.com/nation/2021/02/23/elijah-mcclain-investigation/.
4 Mike Baker, "Before the Death of Manuel Ellis, a Witness Told the Police: 'Stop Hitting Him'," *New York Times*, June 5, 2020, https://www.nytimes.com/2020/06/05/us/manuel-ellis-tacoma-video-unrest.html.
5 Nancy Dillon, "'He Wasn't Resisting Arrest, He Was Trying to Resist Suffocation': Father of Texas Man Who Died in Police Custody," *New York Daily News*, June 13, 2020, https://www.nydailynews.com/news/national/ny-multiple-men-say-i-cant-breathe-before-dying-in-police-custody-20200613-qr7pclr5uff4vnevtz2zy56mxa-story.html.
6 Sarah Deer, "Sovereignty of the Soul: Exploring the Intersection of Rape Law Reform and Federal Indian Law," *Suffolk University Law Review* 38, no. 455 (2005): 456–457, SSRN. A more recent study found that *over one in two* Native American women experiences sexual violence, and ninety-seven percent of female Native American victims of violence report having been the victim of at least one non-Native perpetrator. André B. Rosay, "Violence against American Indian and Alaska Native Women and Men," *NIJ Journal* 277 (2016): 2, 4, https://www.ncjrs.gov/pdffiles1/nij/249822.pdf.
7 "6 Charts Showing Race Gaps within the American Middle Class," Social Mobility Memos, Brookings, last modified October 21, 2016, https://www.brookings.edu/blog/social-mobility-memos/2016/10/21/6-charts-showing-race-gaps-within-the-american-middle-class/.
8 Devah Pager, "The Mark of a Criminal Record," *AJS* 108, no. 5 (March 2003): 958, https://scholar.harvard.edu/files/pager/files/pager_ajs.pdf. Another study found that Asian and Black candidates who "whiten" their resumes – for example by using a Western name instead of an Asian one or by omitting references to Black professional associations were far more likely to get callbacks than those who did not; Asians were nearly twice as likely, and Blacks were two and a half times more likely. Sonia K. Kang, Katherine A. DeCelles, András Tilcsik, and Sora Jun, "Whitened Résumés: Race and Self-Presentation in the Labor Market," *Administrative Science Quarterly* 63, no. 3 (September 2016): 470, https://doi.org/10.1177/0001839216639577.
9 "Rates of Drug Use and Sales, by Race; Rates of Drug Related Criminal Justice Measures, by Race," Effective Government, The Hamilton Project, last modified October 21, 2016, https://www.hamiltonproject.org/charts/rates_of_drug_use_and_sales_by_race_rates_of_drug_related_criminal_justice.
10 "Inside 100 Million Police Traffic Stops: New Evidence of Racial Bias: Stanford Researchers Found That Black and Latino Drivers Were Stopped More Often than White Drivers, Based on Less Evidence of Wrongdoing," *NBC News*, last modified March 13, 2019, https://www.nbcnews.com/news/us-news/inside-100-million-police-traffic-stops-new-evidence-racial-bias-n980556.

Chapter 1

Leading in the wake of an act of explicit racism

Most racism is quiet: A person of color walks into a bank and applies for a mortgage loan. He sits down with a friendly loan officer and fills out the necessary paperwork. A week later, he learns that his application has been denied. Maybe he didn't qualify for a loan. Or maybe he did but was a victim of the unequal treatment that causes non-whites to be more likely to be denied a conventional mortgage than whites of the same socio-economic disposition; more melanin: less chance at a mortgage. Entire communities – Asians, Latinos, Native Americans, and Blacks – have an unjust shot at obtaining the primary asset families use to build generational – and community – wealth: a home, and this phenomenon contributes to large-scale racial inequality.[1] But because no one at the bank used a racial slur, no one wore a white hood, and there was no drama to record on a camera phone, no one is ever likely to know why the application – and so many others – was denied, and if the applicant *does* suspect bias, he's even less likely to be able to prove it.

Quiet.

And yet, sometimes something breaks the silence… a whisper: "I can't breathe," a public official's social media post expressing antebellum sentiment via space age technology, the sight of a police slaying with the aesthetic of a lynching. The most pervasive and powerful forms of prejudice are silent and systemic, and later in this book, I'll address how to fight them, but I'll begin by discussing how to combat explicit bigotry because it is often the racism that we can witness that turns us into warriors.

To illustrate how to employ antiracist strategies in the aftermath of explicit bias, I'm going to provide examples of their usage in the context of an event I and many other people of color have experienced: racial profiling incidents in which community members, security guards, or police accuse non-whites of – or even arrest non-whites for – being somewhere we have every right to be. Acclaimed African American Harvard University Professor Henry Louis Gates, Jr. was arrested by a Cambridge, Massachusetts police officer who believed the scholar to be breaking into his own house. African American Harvard Law Professor Charles Ogletree, former president Barack Obama's mentor, wrote a book inspired by the incident in which he also discussed the

DOI: 10.4324/9781003144298-2

profiling that he and many other African American men had experienced despite the fact that they had significant socio-economic privilege and world-class accomplishments.[2]

People of color of different racial backgrounds and of all walks of life get profiled – two Native American teenagers couldn't even participate in a college tour in peace without a white woman (who mistook them for Latino) calling the police on them – police who, on nothing more than the white woman's false claim that they shouldn't be on the tour, told the teens to put their "hands out" and searched and questioned them.[3] As a woman of color, it happens to me, too. For example, the white concierge of my apartment building questioned me as to my presence there. Another time, a customs official almost refused to let my mother and me enter an entire country, interrogating us for hours. His first question to my mother was, "How can *someone like you* afford to come to New Zealand?" A subsequent question, upon seeing that I had listed my occupation as "student," was, "If you really go to Harvard, name a professor." (He proceeded to conduct an internet search to verify my answer.)

When these incidents happen – when a beloved professor is treated as a criminal or a respected leader, such as Black British Vogue editor-in-chief Edward Enninful, is directed by a security guard to enter his place of work through a loading dock[4] or the police of our cherished campus or alma mater detain guests simply because of their race, it can make us see our organization, community – or country – differently. It forces us to face the fact that all of us aren't treated the same – nor do all of us *treat* people the same. And it invites us to correct what we cannot countenance.

So how do you do that?

Let's imagine that a profiling incident has occurred in your community or organization such as the company where you work, the university or school you attend or are employed by, or the neighborhood in which you live. The first thing to do is investigate.

If you're lucky, your institution or community will conduct an investigation (though all too often, in the wake of an act of explicit racism, *no* formal action is taken), but it will probably limit its exploration to the facts of that specific episode. For example, there may be an inquiry into the security guard who profiled or an interview with the person who was harassed, detained, or arrested. And that's good – the problem is that it is not *enough*.

Explicit racism is the perceptible manifestation of *implicit* systems, and the latter is what *you* have to investigate, because, all too often, incidents of explicit racism are dismissed as one-offs or the actions of bad apples. For example, in the wake of George Floyd's killing, a white public figure told me that the resulting protests were a dysfunctional overreaction to the actions of "one bad police officer" – which is like saying the Civil Rights protests were an overreaction to the actions of "one bad bus driver."

One way to investigate the systemic roots of an act of explicit racism is by conducting an informal inquiry/fact-gathering session. When I was at Yale Law School, one of my Black classmates was studying in the Law School building when a white woman who didn't think she belonged there called a security guard on her. For nothing more than being Black and based on nothing more than a white person's groundless suspicions, the security guard interrogated my classmate about why she was there. When my classmate explained that she was a student, the security guard disbelieved her and forced her to go down the hall to a white professor's office and have him vouch for her. In the wake of multiple such episodes, one of my classmates called a meeting for concerned members of the community.

One participant helped attendees frame the incident in a broader context – Yale is a wealthy, predominantly white university that sits, often uncomfortably, in New Haven, Connecticut, a city with significant poverty and a large Black population. She pointed out that some non-Black Yalies fear poor urban Blacks and anxiously try to distinguish between people of African descent on the town and gown sides of the dichotomy – there was institutional memory of a non-Black professor in the 1970s floating the idea that Black Yale students be made to wear school sweatshirts so non-Black Yale affiliates could distinguish them from New Haven's *other* Black population.

I asked for people to raise their hands if they had been challenged by the security officers who manned the entrance to the Law School building – it turned out several students of African descent had been treated as interlopers. The same school that had replied to our applications by avowing its pleasure to admit us balked at actually letting us through the front door.

One of the attendees informed us that a compendium of the ID photos of the entire student body was available to the security guards; some guards studied the photos, so they could recognize the students they were responsible for protecting. Others didn't bother to expend the effort, instead relying on race as a proxy for determining from whom Yale needed protection.

This kind of information is potent because data combat dismissal. With data – even informal, qualitative data – you are equipped to proceed to the next step: having a radical conversation with your boss, dean, etc. I use "radical" here not in the sense of "extremist" but in the sense of its etymology – radical comes from the Latin "radix" and means "from the root." Armed with data, you can address a problem from the root instead of in a superficial way like *this*:

YOU: Thank you for meeting with me, Dean Johnson. I'm concerned that a security guard interrupted Jane Doe while she was studying and refused to believe she was a student until a white professor vouched for her. There was no reason to think Jane wasn't a student in the first place – she was simply racially stereotyped as a trespasser.

DEAN JOHNSON: Yes, I was extremely dismayed by that, too. But let me assure you that the security guard in question has been disciplined.
YOU: Thank you. I appreciate you taking the incident seriously.

The problem with this kind of dialogue is (a) it doesn't address the fact that the problem goes beyond the behavior of that one security guard, so Black students will continue to be profiled by others on staff, and (b) it doesn't address the racist belief held by some white students and faculty that Black people aren't true members of the community. So, those who hold such beliefs will continue to set guards upon their pupils and peers.

But if you've done the groundwork of conducting your own investigation, you can have a conversation like this:

YOU: Thank you for meeting with me, Dean Johnson. Much of the student body is concerned that a security guard interrupted Jane Doe while she was studying and refused to believe that she was a student until a white professor vouched for her. There was no reason to think Jane wasn't a student in the first place – she was simply racially stereotyped as a trespasser.
DEAN JOHNSON: Yes, I was extremely dismayed by that, too. But let me assure you that the security guard in question has been disciplined.
YOU: Thank you. I really appreciate you taking the incident seriously. However, the problem goes beyond that one security guard. Some of us students, faculty, and staff engaged in an informal inquiry after Jane was profiled, and we learned that students of African descent are routinely profiled by campus security. We think there are a few initial steps the campus could take to remedy that: First, we request that all campus security guards undergo diversity, equity, and inclusion training. Second, we understand that security guards can access and study the student body's ID photos but that only some guards are doing so. We'd like to ask that it be *mandated* that the security guards review ID photos, so they recognize students of *all* colors as such when they enter or move about the building.
DEAN JOHNSON: I had no idea Black students were being suspected by campus security. I just assumed that everyone was being treated the same.
YOU: Unfortunately, that's often not the case, and the problem transcends the behavior of the security staff. Often this Law School is a warm and welcoming place, but too frequently, students and professors, as well as the security guards, treat Black students as though they don't belong – sometimes literally. After all, it was a *student* who began the incident by calling the security guard on Jane.... We'd like to request diversity, equity, and inclusion training for the student body, faculty, and staff as well.

The second dialogue is stronger than the first for two reasons. First, there's power in numbers: You have more of an impact saying "we are concerned" than "I am concerned." (Remember, though, that "we" doesn't have to consist of a large group.) Second, this dialogue focuses not on fixing discrete *problems* but on creating paradigmatic change through proffering *policies*. It deals with *systems* – not *symptoms*.

In the second dialogue, the speaker is direct but gracious – that's important. Many activists condemn "tone policing" – a rhetorical technique in which a privileged person uses the allegedly impolitic tenor of a less privileged person's speech as an excuse to dismiss the latter's advocacy. There is a place in civil discourse for righteous anger, but remember, our goal is to combat racism as effectively as possible and that means being strategic about everything, including in choosing what tone to take. Even if being amicable is not a moral requisite, it can be a tactical move – consider this:

When I attended mediation training at Columbia Law School, the professors led the class in an exercise: Students were partnered and told to sit across from each other on either side of a desk, place their right elbows on the desk's surface, and lock hands. For five minutes, anytime one of the pair got the back of his or her partner's hand to touch the desk, the pair would get a candy. At the end of the minute, the exercise would be over, and the pair could share its winnings.

At first, my partner and I strained as hard as we could to force each other's hands onto the desk – struggling against each other, we earned candies in slow intervals. Then, we grasped the moral of the lesson: Instead of trying to oppose each other, we began rapidly swinging our hands back and forth *in sync*, taking turns touching the backs of our hands to the desk. Now, we were racking up candy.

No one had told us to arm wrestle – we simply "knew" that we were "supposed" to arm wrestle because we had been arranged to engage in a match. Position people to act as adversaries, and they'll play that role. That's why you don't want your demeanor or tone to imply, *My fists are up – you better get yours up, too.* If you're speaking with someone who's fairly decent, invite your interlocutor (the person with whom you're conversing) to partner with you in making the community a more equitable place.

Sometimes, however, it can be tricky to arrive at the first step of engaging in collective inquiry. What if Jane Doe was a member of one minority race, and the security guard a member of another? Let's now describe Jane's background as green, and the security guard's as orange. Imagine that you're orange, too.

YOU: Did you hear about what happened to Jane?
ORANGE COLLEAGUE: Yeah. That was horrible. But the security guard got severely disciplined for making a mistake. White security guards profile green students all the time with impunity, but when an orange security guard does it, he gets a permanent mark put on his record. He's a victim of racism, too. Orange people should be standing with him.
YOU: Should we really be standing with someone who racially profiled?

ORANGE COLLEAGUE: Yeah. Green people don't care about us. In fact, it was green people who robbed my parents' store when they first immigrated from Orangeland. So, why should we spend our time and energy advocating for them?

One of the many roles antiracist leaders can play is rallying people of their own background — whatever it is — to stand in solidarity with those of another: When Nazis began threatening Jews, the Romani, and other minority populations with genocide, it was the Black press that first covered the crisis in America, sounding the alarm that vulnerable people on the other side of the earth were in imminent danger, the first of many actions the Black community would take in solidarity with those targeted by Nazism. Later, during the Civil Rights movement, Jews supported Black causes. Tactically, it makes more sense to fight racism as a multitude than as a minority. But when bigotry is directed against someone who's not of your own race, you may have to face the reality that a significant proportion of people of your race don't care… or even condone it.

If you find yourself in that situation, you can follow the example of a sixty-year-old Hmong American refugee named Youa Vang. When ex-Officer Derek Chauvin, a white man, knelt on George Floyd's neck, ex-Officer Tou Thao, a Hmong American, kept back those who sought to come to Floyd's aid and mocked Floyd as he died.[5] (As of this writing, he has been charged with aiding and abetting second-degree murder and manslaughter.)

To some in the Hmong American community, Floyd's death seemed no more relevant to their people than any other tragedy — as close as the screen in your hand upon which you watched the horrific video, yet so far, far away it might as well have happened in another land or a fictional tale, at once too vivid and too remote to be *real*.[6] Other Hmong Americans reacted with open anti-Black bigotry.[7]

But there were still others like Vang. As I noted, Vang is Hmong. And Vang is a *mom* — a mom to a son who, like Floyd, was killed by the police. When Vang spoke at a Hmong community gathering, this is what she said:

> In this lifetime, there's nothing that could hurt more. He is in my heart every day. I am Fong Lee's mom, and I want to say this to us Hmong people:
>
> I have heard many say, "[B]lack people are bad to us, why must we stand with them?" Let's not think this way. The good are good, and the bad are bad. Even those who are bad are young and just haven't learned to think of others.
>
> We're very few, but when we come together, we are many. We show up for them when they need us, and they show up for us when we need them. Here's what I saw with Fong: Black people were with us the whole time, morning or night.

Whenever we needed something, they were there, even up until one in the morning. We, as Hmong people, must join hands. There aren't many of us. This has brought us so much pain, nothing can compare to it.

So, let's join hands with them. Not to mention our children – we don't want to see this happen to them. We don't want any one of us to ever meet that same fate.[8]

As Vang demonstrates, you can speak both sincerely and strategically. Here are the rhetorical techniques she employs:

First, Vang begins by talking to Hmongs not about Black pain but about *Hmong* pain. *She* could see herself in George Floyd's relatives, but she understood that people who couldn't recognize themselves in Floyd's family would be able to recognize themselves in *her*. Your race is a tool. Your phenotype is a tool. Your story is a tool. Your pain is a tool. Put them to use. If you can interpret between tragedies as others do between tongues, do so if it will serve the cause of justice.

Second, Vang addressed the elephant in the room. She came right out and voiced the realities that some Hmongs stereotyped Blacks as bad – and that some Black individuals *were* bad to Hmongs. Iconic children's television personality Mr. Rogers said, "anything mentionable can be manageable."[9] If there are unfortunate realities to be addressed, *you* mention them, so *you* can manage them. Don't sweep them under the rug in hopes that your adversary won't bring them up – he or she *will*.

Vang managed the difficult parts of the discussion with elegant simplicity – by making the commonsense point that there are good and bad people in every race and that when a Black person is bad, it isn't *because* of race. From her perspective, the behavior of bad individuals was due to a universal cause: immaturity.

Next, Vang appealed to pragmatism: "We're very few, but when we come together, we are many. We show up for them when they need us, and they show up for us when we need them." I imagine Vang intended this statement as affirming altruism. And I'm sure most of her audience took it that way. But if some folks heard, "You scratch my back, and I'll scratch yours," that's fine, too. Some people are motivated by selflessness; others, by self-interest. In a fight against racism, try to animate *both* parties.

And then, near the end of her speech, Vang cast Black people in a new, transformative light by sharing – deploying – the story of how the Black community advocated for Hmongs when Vang's son was killed. If you don't have such a story of the reviled community coming to your community's aid in your personal history, there's likely one in your people's history. There's a lot of do-it-yourself work in antiracist leadership – sometimes you have to play the role of investigator, sometimes that of researcher or professor. If the incident in question involves two populations that have had little previous interaction with each other, a story like the one Vang told may not have happened yet... but you can still find an esteeming story about the people whose dignity you're defending that will have particular resonance with your audience. From slave narratives to the *Diary of Anne Frank*, stories change us – the right anecdote at the right moment can transform.

Vang's speech had a powerful impact not just on the Minneapolis Hmong community but on the world, receiving international attention. Reflecting upon it, I'm reminded of a verse of the Christian Bible that counsels those who seek to do good to be "shrewd as serpents and as innocent as doves." I don't know if Vang would call herself shrewd, but we can shrewdly adopt her tactics.

Remember: Be sincere – but also be savvy.

Let's add another layer of complexity to our hypothetical. Suppose that Jane Doe is orange... and the security guard who profiled her is *also* orange. It happens. After all, another of the ex-officers who aided and abetted ex-Officer Chauvin in killing George Floyd was Black. It's important to understand how intra-racial racism works and to be able to explain it in a way others can understand because you can't fix a problem people don't believe exists.

You need to be able to have this dialogue:

YOU: People in our Law School community are concerned that Jane was racially profiled.
DEAN JOHNSON: Jane wasn't racially profiled – she's orange, and so is the security guard in question.
YOU: People can racially profile others of their background. For example, research shows that Black police officers often face racist pressure from their departments to pick a side – Black or blue – and to demonstrate their loyalty by engaging in racist behavior against Black civilians.[10] The security guard may have felt that if he refused to interrogate Jane as to her presence in the building, then he himself would become the object of suspicion – of his peers. Furthermore, some of us in the community held an information-gathering meeting, and we found that orange students are routinely profiled by campus security. Regardless of the race of the victimizer in this particular instance, the fact that those victimized come so often from one minority group shows that this school is being "secured" in a racist fashion.
DEAN JOHNSON: I just don't know – accusing an orange security guard of profiling an orange student seems like political correctness gone wild.
YOU: I'm not asking you to accuse the security guard. I'm asking you to investigate – interview him as to whether he's ever made a non-orange student have a white professor vouch for her that she's enrolled at the Law School. Ask him if he's approached other students to ask why they were in the building and, if so, what the races of those students were. But mostly, concerned members of our community are requesting that you acknowledge that what happened to Jane might be a manifestation

of our Law School's problem with institutional racism – and that even if it isn't, our inquiry session has revealed that racist security practices are a problem nonetheless. We want the security guard to get due process. But we also want all the security guards to get diversity, equity, and inclusion training, and we request that part of that training address the belief that minority law enforcement and similar professionals need to prove their loyalty to their peers and superiors by mistreating people of their own backgrounds.

★★★

When you organize and issue demands for change, it's important that your plans be SMART: Specific, Measurable, Assignable, Realistic, and Time-related.[11] There is a notorious line from the judicial opinion in *Brown v. Board of Education*, the 1954 U.S. Supreme Court decision that ruled that public school segregation was unconstitutional, directing states to desegregate with "all deliberate speed."[12] Sounds good, right?

The problem is that there's no objective way to gauge the "deliberateness" of someone's speed. If you tell me to run with all deliberate speed, whether I take off at a pace of a four-minute, eight-minute, or eighty-minute mile, you have no way of proving that I am or am not going as fast as I can. The phrase is meaningless. And it allowed segregationists to delay and thwart integration, all the while crossing their fingers behind their backs and swearing that they were moving as fast as possible.

Even when malice isn't involved, it's SMARTness that makes something a goal or plan as opposed to an intention or wish. If you have a leadership role in your organization or community, you may be able to put a plan in place that's completely SMART. If you do not, a perfectly SMART plan may not be feasible – after all, you may lack, for example, the authority to assign the appropriate employee the necessary tasks. But your articulated goal should, nevertheless, be as SMART as possible.

Consider the plan of action the advocate proposed in the above conversation. The plan is Specific: The antiracist asked for a culturally competent investigation of the security guard and diversity, equity, and inclusion training for the security staff as a whole – and not just any training but one that dealt with the realities of being a guard of color. (I'll discuss diversity, equity, and inclusion training and how to employ it effectively in Chapter 3.)

The plan is Measurable in the sense that it can be verified whether or not the requested events have taken place. However, Measurability would be more of a factor if, for example, the antiracist had requested that the security guard staff diversify to the extent that X percentage of the guards were people of color.

In the above scenario, the antiracist doesn't have a position that allows him or her to Assign anyone a task. He or she can't approach the Law School's head of human resources and ask to be presented with a list of diversity, equity, and inclusion consultants in a week, please. However, if Dean Johnson is serious about being not just a school leader but an *antiracist* school leader, *he or she* should Assign each of the necessary tasks so that ideas become action.

The plan the antiracist advocated for is Realistic. Demanding, for example, in December that all the Law School guards will have undergone diversity, equity, and inclusion training by the start of Spring semester so that community members can enter the new year secure in the knowledge that they don't need protection from those who protect them isn't Realistic. Asking that a statement immediately be made that there will be zero tolerance for racial profiling, that a diversity, equity, and inclusion consulting firm be engaged within a month's time, and that training of the security staff begin in the following two weeks *is*.

And that brings us to the last quality of a SMART plan – that it be Time-related. You don't want your community or organization to move ahead with "all deliberate speed." Nor do you want it to *intend* to make changes that then get lost in the shuffle. It's also important not to lose the momentum generated by the backlash to an act of explicit racism. But you don't want measures to be taken in a frenzied and slapdash way, either. Thus, the antiracist leader could have strengthened his or her demands by making them Time-related. Get the agreement to act in place first – then discuss the timing. Putting the whole "ask" into one sentence could bog down the conversation.

In the above situation, the antiracist leader addressed the issue of racist security guards with Dean Johnson. But what about a situation in which the problem *wasn't* security guards? What if Dean Johnson, himself or herself, was the problem?

The moment when a leader in an organization, institution, or community reveals himself or herself to be a bigot through an act of explicit racism can be as jarring as the moment the protagonist of a horror movie realizes her love interest is actually a monster. It's the plot twist we may have never seen coming... or sometimes confirmation of what we've suspected.

Once, I attended a conference put on by a think tank in New Orleans during which speakers discussed how to promote social justice, improve fair trade, and encourage businesses to seek the common good and not just profits. On the afternoon of the second day, an audience member raised her hand to inquire about how people could engage in interfaith efforts to improve society. In the process of making her query she said, "Since many Christians and Muslims have the same values –" That was as far as she got. The speaker, who was one of the leaders of the think tank, interrupted her with a rant that began, "No. No, they *don't*. The way Muslims handle dissent is by chopping heads off...."

Things actually got *worse* from there.

The speaker finished his remarks, and the session was deemed concluded. After the participants filtered out from the hotel conference room – which was decorated, as though by a wry set designer, with paintings of Louisiana plantations – I asked to talk with the speaker privately. Though I wasn't sure how it could be possible, I wanted to check whether he had misspoken. And if, indeed, he had not, I'd hoped that, through civil discourse, I might get him to see how wrong and wrongful his statements had been. But if before it was as though I had glimpsed a swath of white fabric fallen beneath a hem of a coat, now, it was as though the speaker were peering at me through the jack o' lantern eyeholes of a Klansman's hood; his racism was on full display.

By the end of our "discussion," I'd learned for certain that one of the leaders of a powerful and well-resourced think tank, a man who had held prominent roles in the world of national and international politics, helped lead multiple universities, and offered commentary on major news networks and in prominent periodicals held virulently racist views. It sickened me that someone with so much power and influence held reprehensible attitudes, yet I also knew the information I now possessed was like forensic evidence – at once disgusting and useful. I hadn't tried to bait the speaker – my (perhaps pollyannaish) goal had been to persuade. But since persuasion had not been achieved, I'd settle for the consolation prize of *proof*.

This is one reason why, if you're physically present when someone in an organization voices explicitly racist views, engaging the person is a valuable exercise *regardless of the immediate result of the conversation*. If the person misspoke and is responsible enough to offer a correction and apologize, that's a good outcome. If the person *didn't* misspeak but is reachable, that's a good outcome. And if the person didn't misspeak, is bound to his or her beliefs, and uses your conversation to elaborate upon them further, that's good, too. Let the person hold forth until weary. Then, take notes of everything that was said while it's still fresh in your mind. Most bigots are either unaware of or are savvy enough to be stealthy about the animus that influences their actions. If you happen to witness the rare occasions when, like werewolves during the full moon, they reveal their true natures, get proof.

Don't do this at the cost of your personal safety, though – a CEO drunk enough on eggnog to loudly proclaim at the company Christmas party that he or she will never hire a [racial slur] may very well be drunk enough to throw a punch if provoked. In such a context, discreetly observe the situation, take careful notes, and report the comments later to the appropriate party or parties which could include human resources, senior leadership, the board, your union, and/or an attorney (including a legal aid attorney).

Your notes should be as fair and accurate as possible. Document everything both parties said. If you don't remember a certain comment exactly, note that. If you (understandably) lost your temper and escalated the situation in a way that shaped the tenor of your interlocutor's responses, note that. If the person behaved in a manner unbecoming of his or her role, explain *how* he or she did so. "Unbecoming," "disrespectful," and "rude" are conclusions – state whether the person rolled his or her eyes at you, used a sarcastic tone, etc.

Once you've made a record, you have to decide what to do with it. It's best if you aren't obliged to make that decision alone.

As you progress through your antiracist journey, it helps to have someone in your life who can function as a sort of an informal ethics vizier. This is a person who, whether because of vocation or inclination, spends a significant amount of time thinking about how to take ethical action. This person should not merely be someone who is good or upstanding – people can be good without being strategic. Rather, he or she should be someone who is savvy. While your salt of the earth grandpa may tell you, "Well, kiddo, you confronted that jerk – no one can ask more of you than that," your ethics vizier is the one who responds, "It is totally unacceptable for someone with those attitudes to hold that position of power – here are three courses of action you might consider."

The person you tap for advice could be someone with whom you have no personal relationship – for example, a member of your professional organization's ethics committee. Or it could be someone with whom you're on warm terms such as the philosophy professor with whom you stayed in touch. It could be your clergyman who's always involved with social justice work. Almost everyone has someone in his or her life who devotes a lot of time to thinking about what is the right thing to do and how best to do it. But when an act of explicit racism has occurred, and you need to respond promptly, now is not the time to rack your brain for who that person might be. Identify that person *now* for when you need them later. In my situation, I had two people to call upon – two individuals who had served as faculty of the Fellowships at Auschwitz for the Study of Professional Ethics during my fellowship year. They helped me make the first choice one encounters in a situation of this sort: whether to handle things publicly or privately.

On the one hand, remarks made publicly – such as during a conference talk – are fair to attribute publicly to a speaker. (And even private, racist remarks can merit – if not compel – public airing.) Publicizing an incident of explicit racism can warn the world about a bad actor, generate a public conversation that leads to changes beyond the organization or community in which the event occurred, and pressure an institution to make change. If you decide to take this route, you could make a social media post, write an essay for an online publishing platform, or upload footage of the incident. (But before recording a racist incident, be mindful of the relevant laws in your jurisdiction such as whether it is permissible to make an audio tape of someone without their prior consent.) Additionally, you may also want to consult with a lawyer – again, this can be a legal aid lawyer – about protecting yourself from an accusation of libel or slander. But know that, at least in America, traditionally, you can't be liable for defamation if what you say is *true*.

On the other hand, going public can shame – or antagonize – a good institution with a bad actor before that institution has the chance to do the right thing. Depending on the medium you use, you may reach a broad audience but not the powers that be at the institution in question. And, ultimately, by making an institution a talking *point*, you may lose the opportunity to talk *with* it.

I chose to go the private route. I contacted the president of the think tank by email, indicated in the subject line that the matter was of grave importance, and crafted my notes into a formal letter. The president of the organization wrote me back that he would investigate the matter.

Job done?

No.

Being antiracist isn't about doing your good deed for the day – it's about being *effective*. Once I witnessed that act of explicit racism, handling it to the fullest extent that I was capable became my responsibility. Thus, after some time passed, I reached out again to the president of the think tank who informed me that while he couldn't comment directly on personnel issues, he *could* share that the leader had moved on to pursue other opportunities.

Yay!

Martin Luther King once said, "It may be true that the law cannot change the heart, but it can restrain the heartless." As antiracists, we can't always change the heart, but we *can* sometimes restrain the heartless from having platforms or positions for which they are unfit. My initial concern about the bigoted thought leader was not primarily that he was racist – so are a lot of people – but that he was a racist with a gigantic sphere of influence. When the think tank learned the rhetoric that the thought leader was using its conferences to disseminate, it was not interested in continuing to provide a sphere of influence to him.

Some may object that the thought leader was censored or deprived of his right to free speech. Neither of which is the case. He had the right to speak his mind. I had the right to speak mine in response. The think tank had the right to decide what constituted abuse of its platform. And, had I gone public, those who read or heard my reflections would have had the right to decide whether they wanted to support the speaker or the think tank.

If the think tank had decided not to punish the leader for his repugnant statements, then I would have gone public. But that wasn't necessary in this case. By handling things privately and amicably, the thought leader was removed, and the think tank had the sort of positive interaction with an antiracist that serves as a foil to the caricature of the "social justice warrior."

As for the thought leader – he seems to have retreated from the spotlight. But were he to take on a prominent role in the public sphere or politics once again, I would have to consider whether to reveal to his employer – or the world – what he said that day in that New Orleans hotel.

★★★

The story I told above is true but not *complete* – just as most stories of antiracism aren't. It's not complete because though I talked about what I said and what I did, I left out most of what I *felt*.

When I confronted the leader of the think tank, my pulse raced. When he doubled down on his hateful stance, it kindled a quiet fury in me that singed my own insides. When I drafted the letter to the thought leader's employer – which incorporated copious references demonstrating the inaccuracy of the thought leader's statements – I felt harried. The year I attended the conference, I was completing my dissertation and didn't have time to draft an apologia for non-Christian and non-Western civilizations. And when it was all over and I learned the thought leader "had moved on to pursue other opportunities," I felt joyful – and exhausted.

Antiracist work takes a toll, and my own efforts and their costs don't begin to compare to those experienced by historical figures like Rosa Parks and Elizabeth Eckford. The story of Rosa Parks refusing to give up her seat on the bus is famous. But it's rarely talked about how she suffered ulcers.[13] Many of us have seen the picture of Elizabeth Eckford's superhuman stoicism as she and the rest of the Little Rock Nine integrated the Arkansas public school system surrounded by a wild horde of white supremacists. But how many of us are aware that, in the wake of day after day of being punched, kicked, scalded with water, spat on, and having rocks and broken glass thrown at her by her classmates, Eckford would go on to attempt suicide multiple times and to be diagnosed with post-traumatic stress disorder that would not *begin* to heal for almost forty years?[14]

As an antiracist, you must be intentional about taking care of yourself both for your own sake and so you can live to fight another day. I was fortunate to have an extraordinary antiracist in my life who modeled self-care – Täo Porchon-Lynch, who held the Guinness World Records for being the oldest yoga teacher and competitive ballroom dancer, was my instructor, mentor, and friend. When I met her, she was one hundred, and she was thought to be the only living person who'd marched with both Martin Luther King, Jr. and Gandhi – in between, she'd been a Holocaust rescuer. And even in old age, she was *still* an activist.

Täo's whole life was about justice – but not every moment was spent in the pursuit of it. She took time for meditation, for breathing exercises, and for prayer. She cultivated a connoisseurship of wine and got regular manicures. She gave herself breaks – much like an athlete catching his breath on the bench for a bit during a game – and then relaunched herself into the fray, an even more formidable force for having rested.

As many antiracist causes as Täo fought for in over a century of living, even she didn't take on them all. No one can. We have to make choices. When I chose, as a law student, to join the legal team representing Connecticut Coalition for Justice in Education Funding in its suit against the state – which was plagued by the worst achievement gap in the union, I chose *not* to participate in Yale Law's Capital Punishment Clinic, advocating for people who had received the – extremely racially discriminatory[15] – death penalty. If I had tried to contribute to both those rigorous, time-intensive, high-stakes, high-pressure causes, I would have burned out and been unable to do either. At the same time, choosing to do *nothing* can engender a guilt that also debilitates.

Find the balance.

We should *always* be antiracist, but we should be mindful of how we allocate our resources. During some seasons of our lives, we may have time to donate to the quest for racial justice but not money – in others, the reverse might be true. After participating in an initiative to combat the American epidemic of Black maternal mortality,[16] we might pause before taking up the fight against the inequity that results in cystic fibrosis, a genetic disease that primarily affects white Americans, getting three and a half times more research funding from the National Institutes of Health and *440 times* more funding from national research foundations[17] than sickle cell disease, an equally serious genetic illness that primarily affects Black Americans and Hispanic Americans despite the fact that one third fewer Americans have cystic fibrosis than have sickle cell disease.[18] But we pause with the understanding that if we hear a racist remark, we'll challenge it, just as a doctor on a flight to the resort where she's spending vacation will still answer the call if a fellow passenger has an emergency and a flight attendant asks if a physician is on board.

In sum, recognize that, as an antiracist, you are an instrument of justice. Treat that instrument like a Stradivarius.

★★★

Some antiracist work is about speaking truth to power, but much antiracist work is about speaking truth to peers. Institutional racism is an existential threat, but institutions are made up of individuals, and the more those individuals engage in brave and vulnerable conversations with people of character, the more likely they are to act justly themselves. Many antiracist leaders have pointed out that being "colorblind" isn't the most effective way to address prejudice – after all, if you can't see color, you can't see when people are treated differently *because* of color. Too often, what "colorblind" actually means is "racism-blind." But there's an adjunct to being colorblind, and that's what I term being "colormum." While the colorblind person doesn't – or claims not to – see race, the colormum person doesn't discuss it.

However, when an explicitly racist event has transpired on the national – or neighborhood – stage, it's important not to be colormum. Here's why:

First, being colormum sends the message that racism is such a non-issue it isn't worth grieving, that racism is not a tragedy but simply part of quotidian life – when, in fact, it's *both*. Addressing explicit racism when it happens keeps us from becoming inured to or accepting of it. When an act of antisemitic violence happened, I sent condolences to my Jewish loved ones and colleagues, and when George Floyd was killed, my non-Black loved ones and colleagues sent their condolences to me. Proactively demonstrating your care for the people in your community is an important component of serving them as a leader and is a leadership action you can take whether you're the CEO, the intern, or the janitor.

If being colormum is the norm for you, you may feel awkward taking this step. You may wonder what you would say – and to whom you would say it. If a white supremacist group just burned down a house of worship in a green community, and the only green person you know is your cousin's ex-girlfriend, you don't need to reach out to her. But even acquaintances such as the neighbor you chat with from time to time and that co-worker you like but don't know that well will likely appreciate a thoughtful, heartfelt, well-intended comment or note – and if you happen to have real relationships with green people, those individuals almost certainly will.

Your efforts can be as simple as a brief but sincere text or email reading, "Joe, I just heard about how that hate group burned down that green house of worship. I am heartbroken. I want to let you know that the green community is in my thoughts. Sincerely, Name." For the subject line of such emails, I use "In Solidarity."

The type of verbal remarks you should make depends on the nature of your relationship with the person you're addressing. If it's someone you're close to, you might say something similar to the above, preferencing it with a comment such as "Hey, Anna. I know we don't talk about race much, but I just wanted to say...." From there, follow Anna's lead. She may need to vent, or it may be too painful for her to linger on the horror of what happened. If you're speaking to someone you don't know well, you can say, "Hey. How are you doing? I just wanted to let you know I heard about what happened to that green house of worship, and I'm thinking of/praying for you." Even better: "I'm thinking of/praying for you, and I want you to know I [wrote Congressman Smith about the need to devote more resources to stopping hate groups/attended the protest over the suspects not being arrested yet, etc.]." Also good is: "I'm going to look online for ways to help/donate, and if there's anything you happen to know of that I can do, please don't hesitate to let me know."

If the person you're speaking to may have special insights into what help is needed because she has a direct connection to the event – for example, if she was a member of the house of worship that burned down, it's appropriate to ask her what you can do to help. But if the person merely happens to be the same race as the victimized group, there's a fine line between *deferring* to her expertise as an ingroup member and *assigning* her the job of being your personal research assistant while she's already burdened with trying to navigate both the responsibilities of her daily life and her grief. Remember, you may not be green, but you do have access to the internet and/or to news media. You can see for yourself if there's a rebuilding fund to which you can donate or a petition you can sign. If you're going to ask for advice on what you can do, first demonstrate that you've already made an effort to ascertain for yourself what can be done.

The second reason to renounce being colormum – to take a vow *against* silence – is that being colormum prevents you from checking bigoted behavior that occurs within your racial group. People are often most comfortable articulating racist beliefs among those of their own background under the belief that the same skin = the same sentiments. But if there's one benefit to people feeling safe enough around you to say what they really feel and think, it's that you get the opportunity to address those notions.

There's no time off for antiracists – if you're committed to justice, then you have to be committed to addressing racism whenever you encounter it. So, if in the wake of explicit racism – or any other time – someone forwards you a pseudo-intellectual video that blames the victim or texts you a bigoted meme or recruits you to take a stand against those demonstrating for justice (whom they accuse of being the *real* villains of the tale), you have an ethical obligation to say something.

But *how* you say it matters. Engage graciously because even if an objective observer would look at your use of rich historical context, statistics cited to the premier academic journals, witty rhetorical flourishes, and ovation-worthy one-liners and conclude that you won the debate, if your adversary and any likeminded friends and relatives present haven't changed their attitudes – and thus won't change their behaviors, then what did you actually win?

I'll discuss the art of antiracist discussion more in the next chapter, but here are some basic things to keep in mind: First, the most important thing to know about debating is that it isn't always necessary to engage in it. Sometimes, for example, someone might tell a racist joke not because it reflects his worldview but simply because he thinks it's funny. In that situation, nothing more may be required than firmly and concisely reminding the person that such behavior is unacceptable.

The key is to do this in a way that *allows* the joker to understand the inappropriateness of his behavior and change it rather than *antagonizes* him into digging in and hardening his position. There are a couple of simple tricks that can help you do this – psychology professor Kevin Nadal's suggestions on how those targeted by racism can respond can be adapted by those who don't wish to be bystanders to bigotry. Nadal counsels those challenging a racial statement to speak in the first rather than the second person to avoid putting the person being corrected on the defensive – "*I* feel disappointed that you would tell a joke like that" is more likely to be effective than "*You're* racist to tell such a joke." Furthermore, explaining how we feel can help the other person understand the impact of his or her words. He also advises "to address the behavior and not the perpetrator," i.e. "that *joke* was racist" will go over better than "*you* are racist."[19] Other times, someone may make a prejudiced remark in seriousness, and yet, you understand the comment to be beneath the person. In other words, the individual's statement, while profoundly wrong, is also uncharacteristic. In a situation in which you're dealing with someone who's normally decent, just resolutely but graciously – and succinctly – correct the fallacy behind the remark. For example, on a Thanksgiving Day, a Black family friend mentioned that she sometimes felt frightened by seeing people in Muslim garb because she felt such regalia might indicate terroristic tendencies. I replied that the media often frames non-white races or religions associated with them in bigoted fashion, portraying Arab, Persian, and Central and South Asian Muslims as terrorists and Blacks as criminals, but we could use our firsthand knowledge of the unfairness of the latter stereotype to extrapolate to the unfairness of the former. I also observed that, as a Black person, I was confident that white supremacy had probably posed more of a threat to her than terrorism committed by those warping Islam.

There are a few techniques I employed here. First, I made the media, not my family's friend, the ultimate bad guy. Yes, my friend is a hundred percent responsible for her attitudes. But if you want someone to exit racism, it can help to give them a graceful out. Second, like Youa Vang, I used bigotry against my friend's and my own race as a lens through which to view bigotry toward the racialized group she had stereotyped. Third, I didn't try to be the authority – I let her use her *own* experience as the authority. I knew that this high-powered Black woman would have had experiences such as being pulled over by a cop who questioned her as to where she had gotten her luxury car or being followed around the upscale stores where she shopped by salespeople who regarded her as a potential shoplifter – and I was almost certain that the people who had done such things hadn't been wearing hijabs or taqiyahs.

Every day, intelligent-sounding, rational-seeming people appear on our screens and in our social media feeds, and tell us to hate or fear or look down on various non-white peoples. And every now and then, something they say – especially if it gets repeated often enough – can penetrate. When that happens, a conversational correction that has the vibe of "I respect you as a reasonable person, thus I'm going to reason with you" shouldn't feel like an attack to the person you're addressing. It's likely to be enough to bring the person back to themselves, to the upstanding human being you know them to be. Say your piece with firmness and *humility*, and then don't drop the mic – just pass the peas.

Sometimes, however, addressing racism can be a little more... involved....

Sometimes racism is like a dandelion – a prejudiced sentiment whose seeds blew onto some unfortunately fertile soil and took root *but* whose sprouts can be easily plucked out. On the other hand, sometimes racism is like a rosebush – it's cultivated and deeply rooted, and, if you try to pull it out, you're likely to be pierced by thorns.

Go for it anyways.

Abolitionist William Lloyd Garrison explained his strategy for trying to convert those who were pro-slavery as follows: "With reasonable men, I will reason; with humane men I will plead; but to tyrants I will give no quarter, nor waste arguments where they will certainly be lost." This approach works not just when someone makes a graphically racist remark but when someone makes a willfully blind one like: "There's no racism in policing." If the person is "reasonable," or what might be colloquially termed "left-brained," cite to facts and statistics. Point out, for example, the *Washington Post* study that found that unarmed Black men are about four times more likely than unarmed white men to be shot by the police.[20] If the person is humane or "right-brained," plead by telling a story from your life or from the life of one of your loved ones that might carry more weight than cold statistics. For example, I sometimes tell the true story of how my father was once walking up the driveway to my grandparents' home in broad daylight and almost got arrested by the police because they thought he was a robber. I explain the indignity of my father having to submit to those police officers so as not to be accused of resisting arrest. I invite my conversation partner to empathize with what it feels like to have to acquiesce to police officers no matter how oppressive or unfair their behavior is.

But the last part of Garrison's strategy is equally important – there's a proverb that you can't wake up someone who's pretending to be asleep. If you're in such a conversation, stop and allocate your finite resources of time and energy toward something that's productive.

Make the decision to exchange being colormum for being a professional antiracist. By that, I don't mean become a fulltime antiracist activist like Martin Luther King, Jr. – I mean bring antiracism into your vocation or avocation. In Charles Dickens' *A Christmas Carol*, the ghost of Scrooge's late business partner Jacob Marley says that his life was a failure. Scrooge is stunned by Marley's self-assessment and protests that Marley was "a good man of business":

> "Business!" cried the Ghost, wringing its hands again. "Mankind was my business. The common welfare was my business; charity, mercy, forbearance, and benevolence, were, all, my business. The dealings of my trade were but a drop of water in the comprehensive ocean of my business!"[21]

If you want a just world, that has to be your attitude, too. Antiracism has to be your business. The good thing is that antiracism is like sea salt – you can sprinkle it onto pretty much anything and make that thing better.

Antiracism can be the theme of the meditation presented at the end of a yoga teacher's class, a clergyman's sermon, a volunteer's Sunday School lesson, or a co-ed's Bible study. It can inspire a book club selection or the choice of literature a teacher has his or her students read. But it's easy to forget this. We can become so used to the marginalization of people who aren't white that we think of discussion of them and their struggles for justice as necessitating a special occasion or only being appropriate in certain contexts, at specific times of the year. Sometimes, even the very right of non-white people to exist and to do so with dignity is labeled political, controversial, or divisive. Yet, while antiracism is often constricted to certain dedicated spaces and times, racism afflicts non-whites in every domain of life without respite. So, if you have an opportunity to speak out or educate in the aftermath of an act of explicit racism, do so, whether it's to a lecture hall of hundreds of college students or the half dozen friends gathered in your living room for your wine and romance novel club. (Yes, there are even romance novels involving passionate heroes and heroines of color that, while not "about" racism, deal with the subject.) And keep speaking out or educating regularly until the world is racially just, until this earth is finally worthy of our children.

You don't have to wait for a History Month, an ethnic holiday, permission from your superiors, or a prompt from your curriculum to do so. You can get crazy and teach Black history *outside of February*. Plays about the indigenous people can deal with other subjects than the (heavily fictionalized) first Thanksgiving and can be put on not just by elementary schools but by professional theater companies. It isn't anti-white to regularly remind yourself that *white is not the default*. People of color are people. All people have problems. Some of the problems people of color experience come from racism. Teach, preach, and lead from that perspective.

And when you're tempted to be colormum remember: Awkward is better than evil. By that I mean the awkwardness of talking about race can be deeply uncomfortable, but it's infinitely preferable to the evil that flourishes when we keep silent. And keep in mind that talking about race is awkward at first for the same reason holding a pencil, swinging a golf club, or riding a horse is awkward at first – because you haven't gotten accustomed to it. As with any other practice, the more you talk about race, the more natural it will become for you.

For my twenty-first birthday, my mother and I took a girls' trip to London. We had just finished eating a dinner of fish and chips, when the white, middle-aged, English couple at the next table turned to us. They said they had noticed our American accents and had some questions for us about race in America. And from there, with complete strangers, my mother and I ended up having a long, candid conversation about an extremely sensitive subject that was more heartfelt and forthright than any discussion of race I'd ever had with my white loved ones.

I remember them asking us why, when they watched episodes of a popular American court TV show that was broadcast internationally, the Black plaintiffs and defendants always seemed to have disreputable personal histories. I explained how representations of Black people in the media aren't reflective of our realities. For example, a study of media portrayals of Black men (that came out after my London visit) by The Opportunity Agenda found that negative associations such as criminality, unemployment, and poverty were exaggerated while positive associations were limited – Black men were generally depicted in a positive light only in the context of athleticism, musicality, or masculinity and not in the context of virtues.[22] I remember how *relieved* the couple was. In their hearts, they knew that the way Black people were depicted on the program they watched wasn't accurate... and *yet*, night after night, one specimen of Black dysfunction after another was presented to their bewildered gazes.

They asked my mother and me if racism was still really a problem in America. Many white people believe that the absence of "whites only" signs translates to the absence of "whites only" attitudes. I explained to the couple how a white friend's mother who adored me, lovingly welcoming me into her home, and tucking me in with a goodnight kiss at slumber parties from the time I was a little girl, told my mother that when the prep school her daughter and I attended held a formal dance to which girls invite boys, that I should invite a Black boy or, if I didn't know any socially – as there were none in our grade – I should invite a cousin so that no one would feel "uncomfortable." Mind you, this was not in the pre-Civil Rights era. I'm a millennial.

I'm not suggesting anyone go so far as to approach a stranger of a different background and ask to start a conversation about racism (although I've actually had other people – of diverse backgrounds – approach me for conversations like this, and it's always been a respectful and positive experience), but I offer that example to illustrate that people are far freer to discuss race across race than they imagine themselves to be.

Finally, remember that sometimes the occasions when you're most tempted to be colormum are when it's most important to speak. In the wake of an act of explicit racism, there are often fraught conversations in institutions and communities. And you may find, in the speech or silences of those who surround you, a disconcerting indifference, willful blindness, or even an unambiguous hate. When that happens, someone needs to lead to move people to a place of compassion and ethical responsibility. And one way to do that is by disclosing your status as a victim of racism... or witness of it... or perpetrator of it.

Racism was invisible to one of my white friends until she saw the video of ex-Officer Chauvin kneeling on George Floyd's neck. She called me crying from grief and from the strain of cognitive dissonance: "I thought we were past this," she said. After all, America elected a Black president. "Surely, you aren't subject to racism," she said. "You practice law at an elite firm and have Ivy League degrees."

Listening to her, I realized something – as in any friendship, this woman and I shared our joys and sorrows with each other. When she asked me how my week went, I might tell her about an incredible museum exhibit I visited or discuss my worry over an elderly relative's health. But I'd *never* tell her that the white concierge in my apartment building stopped me as I entered and rudely interrogated me as to whether I lived there. I wouldn't tell her how, while walking around my neighborhood on a sunny evening, a white man pulled over in a luxury convertible and questioned me and my presence there.

I wouldn't tell her how the rideshare driver asked what I did for a living, and, when I told him I was an attorney, scoffed, "You mean a paralegal?" I wouldn't tell her how I was mistaken for a secretary at my office. I wouldn't tell her how, when getting turned around on my way to visit a friend who lives in a tony, white neighborhood, I pulled over at a stop sign to ask a white pedestrian for directions, and he wouldn't answer me. He didn't walk away from me. He just silently leveled a long, hate-filled stare at me until I drove away. I wouldn't tell her. I wouldn't tell her. I wouldn't tell her.

But in our conversation about Floyd, I learned that because I didn't tell my white friend about the racism I experience, she assumed that I *don't* experience it. By having a friendship dynamic in which I shared my joys and my pains – except for the ones I suffered due to prejudice, my friend came to believe that racism was no longer a serious problem in our country because the Black person she loved the most didn't seem to experience it. Worse, my silence became a counter to evidence of racism proffered by others. Because I hadn't disclosed the ways that racism effects #metoo, my compassionate, white friend, entirely absent malice, turned me into a mental hashtag: #butshannon. "Yes, John Doe said racism is a problem, but Shannon is Black, and she has a Harvard doctorate. Yes, Jane Doe told me racism is still prevalent, but Shannon is a lawyer at a top firm, so how prevalent can it be? Yes, John Smith described to me an encounter he had with a bigot, but Shannon never mentions such experiences, so he must have misperceived the interaction."

So, I resolved that from then on, I was going to tell my white loved ones when I suffered racism just as they and I tell each other about our other sufferings. I'm a person of color. Some of the pain I experience in this life comes from racism. I decided I wasn't going to be silent about that anymore.

The anti-sexual harassment movement has #metoo. I think the antiracism movement should be inspired by the title of Langston Hughes' poem "I, Too." Though your race may be obvious, the bigotry you experience may not be. Thus, there's power in self-disclosing that #Itoo am a survivor of racism. Listeners who may not be swayed by a talking head, an academic, a politician, or an athlete may be moved – and moved to action – by someone with whom they're intimate, or even just familiar, sharing his or her story.

But the #Itoo ethos isn't just for non-whites. I'll never forget when a white acquaintance, a young woman of my own age, shared an experience she'd had in upper school: It was popular for teenagers in her town to drive to a particular off limits, out of the way area to hang out at night. One night, she had driven out with two Black guys from her class, and the three of them were sitting in the car talking when a white adult caught them. After gesturing for my acquaintance to roll down the window, the adult asked, "Are you all right?" My acquaintance said that she was. Then the woman asked her, "Did they rape you?"

My acquaintance's reaction was to laugh, so stunned was she by the dark outlandishness of the question. "Did they rape you?" the woman asked again, this time more insistently. My acquaintance told the truth: no. She was in shock as the woman left. Her friends told her *they* were in shock that she hadn't falsely accused them to get out of trouble. She was further stunned that the guys weren't surprised by the woman's preposterous but dangerous question and wouldn't have been surprised if my acquaintance had played into the woman's prejudices. *I* was stunned that my acquaintance was sharing the story with *me*.

That's because no matter how much quantitative or qualitative data about racism we marshal, many white people try to make people of color feel that we're delusional about its existence. I wasn't used to white people acknowledging racism from the perspective of their whiteness. I had experienced plenty of white people arguing that racism didn't exist – or that the *real* racism was directed against *them*. What I had very rarely experienced was a white person, speaking with the authority that white privilege unjustly but undeniably confers, saying, #Itoo can vouch for the existence of racial prejudice.

Sometimes, when people of color discuss racism, white people's prejudices distort the message: Legitimate expressions of sufferings are received as cynical deployments of grievance. Someone's appropriate anguish is perceived as irrational anger. But when a white person speaks to other white people about racism or when green people talk to other green people about the prejudice faced by orange people, as members of the ingroup, they have a good chance of getting past the defenses that would be raised against members of the outgroup.

When you make a #Itoo statement among people of your background, it's a way of signaling that you're going to get real. Your vulnerability in revisiting the pain of an experience you witnessed – or the guilt of an incident in which you were the perpetrator – invites others to become similarly vulnerable and to be honest with themselves about what they've tried not to see or believe or admit.

One thing is for certain: If we don't come forward to describe our realities, our silence will be used to furnish others' fictions.

And when you have to go beyond describing to debating… that's the subject of Chapter 2.

Notes

1 Emmanuel Martinez and Aaron Glantz, *How Reveal Identified Lending Disparities in Federal Mortgage Data* (Emeryville, CA: Reveal from the Center for Investigative Reporting, 2018), https://s3-us-west-2.amazonaws.com/revealnews.org/uploads/lending_disparities_whitepaper_180214.pdf.
2 See Charles Ogletree, *The Presumption of Guilt* (New York: Palgrave Macmillan, 2012).
3 Sam Levin, "'They Don't Belong': Police Called on Native American Teens on College Tour," *The Guardian*, May 4, 2018, https://www.theguardian.com/us-news/2018/may/04/native-american-students-colorado-state-college-tour-

police; Sarah Hinger, "2 Native American Teens Were Reported to Police for Joining a Campus Tour. Now We're Stepping In," *American Civil Liberties Union*, September 20, 2018, https://www.aclu.org/blog/racial-justice/race-and-inequality-education/2-native-american-teens-were-reported-police.

4 Oscar Holland, "British Vogue Editor Was 'Racially Profiled' by Security Guard at Magazine's Offices," *CNN style*, July 16, 2020, https://www.cnn.com/style/article/edward-enninful-vogue-racially-profiled/index.html.

5 Jeff Baenen / AP, "New Police Body Camera Footage Captures Onlookers' Horror during Fatal Arrest of George Floyd," *Time*, August 14, 2020, https://time.com/5879689/tou-thao-body-camera-floyd-arrest/.

6 Chris Fuchs, "Hmong Family Whose Son Was Shot by White Officer Speaking Out in Solidarity," *NBC News*, June 2, 2020, https://www.nbcnews.com/news/asian-america/hmong-family-whose-son-was-shot-white-officer-speaking-out-n1222281.

7 Jessica Lussenhop, "George Floyd Death: 'The Same Happened to My Son'," *BBC*, June 15, 2020, https://www.bbc.com/news/world-us-canada-53023703.

8 Ryan General, "Mom of Hmong Teen Killed by Minneapolis Cop in 2006 Voices Support for BLM," *NextShark*, June 2, 2020, https://nextshark.com/fong-lee-minneapolis-cop-blm/.

9 Alyson Walls and Mark Houser, "Mr. Rogers Would Want Parents to Explain Death," *Trib Live*, February 28, 2003, https://archive.triblive.com/news/mr-rogers-would-want-parents-to-explain-death/.

10 Jennifer E. Cobbina, *Hands Up Don't Shoot: Why the Protests in Ferguson and Baltimore Matter, and How They Changed America* (New York: New York University Press, 2019), 56.

11 George T. Doran, "There's a S.M.A.R.T. way to write management's goals and objectives," *Management Review* 70, no. 1 (November 1981): 36, EBSCO.

12 "With All Deliberate Speed," Separate Is Not Equal: Brown v. Board of Education, Smithsonian National Museum of American History Behring Center, September 15, 2020, https://americanhistory.si.edu/brown/history/6-legacy/deliberate-speed.html.

13 Jeanne Theoharis, "The Real Rosa Parks Story Is Better Than the Fairy Tale," *New York Times*, February 1, 2021, https://www.nytimes.com/2021/02/01/opinion/rosa-parks.html.

14 David Margolick, "Through a Lens, Darkly," *Vanity Fair*, September 24, 2007, https://www.vanityfair.com/news/2007/09/littlerock200709; Dan Grossman, "After 50 Years of Silence, Member of Little Rock Nine Opens Up about Harrowing Experience," *TheDenverChannel.com*, June 30, 2020, https://www.thedenverchannel.com/news/america-in-crisis/after-50-years-of-silence-member-of-little-rock-nine-opens-up-about-harrowing-experience.

15 David A. Love, "The Racial Bias of the US Death Penalty," *Guardian*, January 3, 2021, https://www.theguardian.com/commentisfree/cifamerica/2012/jan/03/racial-bias-us-death-penalty.

16 Angélica Marie Pagán, Vanessa Quintana, and Jenine Spotnitz, "Spring 2020 Journal: Mitigating Black Maternal Mortality," *Berkeley Public Policy Journal*, April 13, 2020, https://bppj.berkeley.edu/2020/04/13/spring-2020-journal-mitigating-black-maternal-mortality/.

17 Alexandra Power-Hays and Patrick T. McGann, "When Actions Speak Louder Than Words – Racism and Sickle Cell Disease," *The New England Journal of Medicine* 383, no. 20 (December 2020): 1902, https://doi.org/10.1056/NEJMp2022125; LaTasha Lee, Kim Smith-Whitely, Sonja Banks, and Gary Puckrein, "Reducing

Health Care Disparities in Sickle Cell Disease: A Review," *Public Health Reports* 134, no. 6 (2019): 599, https://doi.org/10.1177/0033354919881438.
18 Ibid.
19 Kevin L. Nadal, "A Guide to Responding to Microaggressions," *CUNY Forum* 2, no. 1 (2014): 74, https://advancingjustice-la.org/sites/default/files/ELAMICRO%20A_Guide_to_Responding_to_Microaggressions.pdf.
20 Joe Fox, Adrian Blanco, Jennifer Jenkins, Julie Tate, and Wesley Lowery, "What We've Learned about Police Shootings 5 Years after Ferguson," *The Washington Post*, August 9, 2019, https://www.washingtonpost.com/nation/2019/08/09/what-weve-learned-about-police-shootings-years-after-ferguson/?arc404=true.
21 Charles Dickens, *A Christmas Carol: A Ghost Story of Christmas* (London: Chapman & Hall, 1843), Marley's Ghost, http://www.gutenberg.org/files/46/46-h/46-h.htm.
22 Topos Partnership with consultation from Janet Dewart Bell and Eleni Delimpaltadaki Janis of The Opportunity Agenda, *Media Representations and Impact on the Lives of Black Men and Boys* (New York City: The Opportunity Agenda, 2011), https://www.racialequitytools.org/resourcefiles/Media-Impact-onLives-of-Black-Men-and-Boys-OppAgenda.pdf.

Chapter 2

Antiracism rhetorical chess
How to discuss and debate racism effectively

Learning to discuss and debate racism effectively is like learning to shoot layups or bowl strikes – while no approach can make your every attempt successful, there *are* techniques that will dramatically improve your abilities. Strategy-free conversations about racism often combine the awkwardness of teaching children about the birds and the bees with the fruitlessness of trying to convince someone that his or her religious beliefs are wrong. But if you enter a dialogue about race equipped with *tactics*, you'll find that it *is* possible to open and even change peoples' minds on the subject.

Often before you can have a conversation about a racial issue, you must engage in a meta-conversation about the appropriateness of discussing racism at all. Your interlocutor will commonly challenge you in one of the two following ways. First, he or she may argue that the perceived voluminous attention to race and the ubiquity of conversations about it must mean that the issue is overblown. Second, he or she may claim that non-whites who discuss race or advocate for racial justice are wallowing in victimhood.

If your conversation partner takes the first tact and argues, "You see racism everywhere," you can respond with a metaphor:

> Suppose you entered your children's room to find that they had engaged in a pillow fight, and now, down covers the beds, the dresser, the floor, etc. You ask your children to clean up the mess, but when you come in to inspect, you find – and point out – feathers under the bed, on the windowsill, and clinging to the lampshade. You come back a second time, and more feathers are snagged on teddy bear fur and alit upon picture frames. On your third visit, you find still more plumes. It wouldn't make sense for your children to object in exasperation, "You see down *everywhere*." Is it frustrating that down is everywhere? Yes. Is it burdensome cleaning all those feathers up? Of course. But are you at fault for *seeing* down everywhere or is the situation your kids' fault for *getting* it everywhere?

Antiracists see racism everywhere because racism *is* everywhere – facts, such as those cited throughout this book, prove that. It's everywhere that racists put it. And while the person you're speaking with may not have made the

DOI: 10.4324/9781003144298-3

mess, we're *all* responsible for cleaning it up. A moral person finds the omnipresence of racism – not the antiracists seeking to address it – intolerable.

When I employ a metaphor like the one above or use the other language "scripted" in this book, I know the devil is in the delivery. I often speak to my interlocutor like an expert briefing a politician – I treat the situation as that of one intelligent person respectfully sharing information and perspective with another. It can feel maddening and unfair to accord someone respect he or she may not have earned, but if you speak condescendingly, your listener may feel that you are dumbing something down for someone who's both bad and not very bright (even though that is not necessarily your actual viewpoint). This may trigger defensiveness and resistance. Those reactions may not be justified... but they *are* human nature. And they're an obstacle to advocating effectively for the oppressed. After all, if you truly believed someone was not intelligent or potentially moral enough to understand your perspective, you probably would not be working so hard to try to connect and engage with them. Your efforts at antiracism can be seen as a "gift" to individuals you respect enough to want to communicate with them.

If your interlocutor takes the second tact and argues that to condemn and seek to eradicate bigotry is victim-mongering, you can respond with a metaphor as well. You can point out the sick parallel that the lies child predators use to manipulate their victims into silence are often truths when it comes to how people react to testimony about racism: that is, "No one will believe you, and if you tell, you'll be seen as the bad guy."

Ask your interlocutor which is more akin to wallowing in victimhood: passively accepting injustice or taking the initiative to address and combat it? Ask also if victimhood is a mentality or a reality? For example, if someone gets mugged and calls the police to report being a victim of crime, is that person indulging in a shameful, responsibility-shirking victim *mentality* or simply acknowledging a *reality*?

Once you've defended the legitimacy of talking about racism, you can move on to *talking* about racism. When engaging in a contentious discussion about racism, use the two-step technique of Acknowledge, Address. When you discuss racism with someone adverse to you, it's important to acknowledge his or her perspective. Acknowledge does not mean *validate*. It means note. One of your catchphrases needs to be, "So, what I hear you saying is...." Be sure to complete the sentence with a characterization of your interlocutor's position that reflects how she or he would frame it. In other words, if you're engaged in one of the most common antiracism activities – advocating for more diversity at your institution – and your conversation partner disagrees with you, don't scoff, "So, what I hear you saying is basically 'segregation now, segregation tomorrow, segregation forever!'"

(Unless your organization is, for example, a country club that doesn't admit people of certain races and that *is*, in fact, what the person is saying. But even in that context, sarcasm won't serve you.)

Instead, a better summation is something like, "So, what I hear you saying is that you feel we should seek to hire the best qualified candidates in a race-neutral way." If the person responds that that's *not* what he or she is saying, don't move forward in the conversation until you understand and can articulate his or her perspective.

There are two reasons to do this. First, accurately hearing and fairly characterizing someone's view is an act of respect that earns you rhetorical capital even from someone with whom you're disagreeing. Second, if you understand someone's argument – as opposed to a caricature of it – you can offer a more congruent response.

For example, suppose that the situation in which you're advocating for more diversity is one in which you are a healthcare provider at a healthcare facility. It might be appropriate to make any of the following responses:

"So, what I hear you saying is that while diversity is nice, it doesn't really impact the care we provide to our patients." To that, you could cite to the George Mason University study that found that Black newborns, plagued by infant mortality, are three times more likely to die when cared for by white doctors than by Black doctors. (Whether a white infant had a white or Black doctor did not affect its likelihood of dying.)[1] Understanding the other party's position allows you to squarely rebut the notion that diversity is merely a cosmetic frill.

Or your response might be, "So, what I hear you saying is that the bottom line is, no matter one's skin color, everyone reads a blood pressure machine the same way." To this type of comment, you could respond:

> The reason we should affirmatively seek to hire people of color is not because they have some special cultural technique for reading a blood pressure machine but because people of color have been unfairly denied opportunity in the field [and/or at this institution] in the past, and justice requires that this be rectified.

Such a response addresses the fallacy that diversity is only an imperative if diverse populations bring diverse skills to the table.

Or your response might be, "So, what I hear you saying is that instead of focusing on racial diversity, we should focus on ideological diversity – we need a better mix of doctors who have different perspectives on treating cancer." To that, you could respond:

> First, we can pursue *both* racial and ideological diversity. Second, racial diversity and ideological diversity are different because the former is a justice issue, while the latter is not. Sometimes, one perspective will prevail over another because it competes better in the marketplace of ideas. But people were never confined to "war relocation centers," death marched to reservations, or lynched because of the method of cancer treatment they championed. However, the same racism that *did* lead to

those atrocities is why non-whites have faced and continue to face de jure and de facto barriers to employment in the healthcare field,[2] and why there is an ethical imperative to redress employment discrimination.

Variations on this reply can be used to rebut other arguments that non-racial forms of diversity be pursued at the expense of racial diversity.

Or your response might be:

> So, what I hear you saying is that while there's a lot of talk about racial diversity, our employees disproportionately graduated from elite universities. You think we should recognize that people from many different educational backgrounds have great things to contribute.

As with the previous response, there is something you can and should agree with here – your argument isn't with the idea that non-elite universities have gifted graduates, it's with the weaponization of that belief against racial justice. Thus, you can assert that the institution can pursue both goals. You can also acknowledge, though, that graduating from an elite school *does* say something significant about one's training and abilities; thus, an organization that hires non-whites from selective universities over whites from less selective universities is not being discriminatory. In fact, the non-white employees at *your* organization may have graduated from higher ranked universities than their white peers because people of color must work – as the saying goes – twice as hard to get half as far. You might remind your interlocutor that if the organization decides to expand the pool of universities whose graduates it hires, it is important that it do so across the board and be prepared to defend the right of all such hires to be on staff. In other words, a white employee hired from a less selective school should not be championed as an avatar of academic diversity, while a non-white employee from a similar school would either not be considered or, if hired, snubbed for taking a job from a more deserving white candidate.

Or a congruent response might be, "So, what I hear you saying is that there are other forms of demographic oppression than race, so racial diversity shouldn't distract from, for example, giving people of different genders and disabilities opportunity." To this, you could say:

> We absolutely need to address injustices such as sexism and ableism. But if we don't address them *alongside* racism, then we're just giving white supremacy a hip, diverse makeover. If diversity only means that a white woman and a white deaf person get a seat at the table next to the white, able-bodied male, then power continues to be consolidated along racial lines and tangible and non-tangible resources in the form of salaries, benefits, stock options, networking opportunities, etc. remain confined to white households and communities, contributing to the racial wealth gap. Ultimately, pursuing racial diversity in no way compromises our ability to pursue gender

and ability diversity – after all, non-white people come in different genders and have disabilities.

Another technique you can use in conversation about race and racism is Pulling off the Invisibility Cloak. In the folklore, fairy tales, and literature of many cultures, invisibility cloaks have the power to hide people and things from view. Racism also serves to render certain facts of life invisible, which can skew the perspective of well-meaning people. For example, a person might ask in good faith, "Why should race be considered in college admissions? Isn't it fairer to just judge applicants in a purely meritocratic way?" The person who poses this question is assuming that standardized test scores, grades, and other quantitative factors truly measure merit – and, if they did, the answer to the question might be "yes." But your job, in this context, is to snatch away the cloak that renders invisible the racialized injustices that make some college applicants appear objectively more meritorious than others.

Take standardized tests and grades for example. It would appear that the candidate with the higher scores is the more meritorious. But at the predominantly white upper school I attended, when a student wanted an aid to achieve the scores he or she (or the student's parents) wanted on a quiz, exam, or standardized test, the student would commonly go through the expensive process of getting a psychologist to say that the student needed disability accommodations. Students could suddenly, in their teens, be declared disabled and granted more time. And the College Board and the American College Testing organization don't disclose the fact to admissions offices.[3]

White students are more likely to have a "504 plan" (named for Section 504 of the U.S. Rehabilitation Act of 1973) that grants them extended time on tests than students of any other race.[4] But unlike an applicant from an underrepresented minority who is assumed to have been the beneficiary of affirmative action, the head start the white student got is invisible.

And that's just *one* head start. Non-white school districts get $23 *billion* less funding than white school districts despite serving the same number of students.[5] Elite colleges prefer students who excelled in advanced classes, but Black, Hispanic, and Native American students are often deprived of the chance to shine in such courses because they're less likely than their white counterparts to attend high schools that even *offer* them.[6] But non-white children *are* more likely to have their credentials tarnished – for example, African American girls are nearly six times more likely to get out-of-school suspensions than white girls *even though they don't behave worse or misbehave more often than them.*[7] I could go on and on.

When race is considered in college admissions, it's an attempt to correct for those disparities on the back end. But people who say that race should *not* be considered – only merit – may not see that. From their perspective, they're making the reasonable and fair argument that, in a race, the only thing that should matter is who crossed the finish line first. The fallacy of that view, however, is that you can't tell whether the runner who crossed the finish line first is more meritorious than her competitor if you don't also look at *whether she got a head start.*

In our society, the sight of the runners crossing the finish line is visible. The sight of the referee tugging the finish line ribbon closer to the runner of color is visible. The sight of the great big head start that the white runner got is utterly invisible.

Pull off the invisibility cloak.

Of course, you can't pull off the invisibility cloak if you aren't aware that anything has been hidden from view. And, unfortunately, most schools fail to teach the history, sociology, and other disciplinary knowledge that explains how racism shapes every aspect of our lives (which is a fact that should be noted to interlocutors as it provides listeners of goodwill an opportunity to learn and change without totally losing face by giving them the chance to realize that their lack of awareness was part of the source of their previous attitudes or positions). But where there's smoke, there's fire, and where there's racial disparity, there's usually racial discrimination. Do the research, so you can uncover and expose that discrimination.

But let's go back to one of the examples I gave of educational inequity – the difference in the out-of-school suspension rates of Black and white girls. Sometimes, when trying to call attention to injustice, antiracists simply state something like, "Black girls receive six times the out-of-school suspensions as white girls." The point antiracists *think* they are making is that schools treat Black girls unfairly. However, it doesn't necessarily follow that just because girls of one race are disproportionately disciplined that unfairness is to blame. And your interlocutor may very well conclude that Black girls are just six times as bad as white ones. The person you're speaking with may think, "Racial disparity does not equal racial injustice. Is this person suggesting it's racist to discipline Black girls more frequently than white girls even if Black girls misbehave more frequently than white girls?" Because many people mistakenly believe that antiracist activism is an attempt to confer upon non-white people equal benefits despite disparities in merit and to see that no non-white race is ever penalized more than whites even if some races have a higher rate of transgression, your conversation partner may very well interpret your comments in this manner. Thus, when you throw out a statistic such as that Black girls get six times the out-of-school suspensions as white girls, *it is crucial that you also note the rest of the fact* – for example, that this happens even though Black girls do not misbehave worse or more frequently than white girls.[8] As a presenter at an NAACP LDF Annual Airlie Civil Rights Training Conference I once attended explained, presenting your interlocutor with incomplete facts can actually *entrench* racism.

Another technique to employ when discussing or debating racism is Recognizing and Addressing Solipsism. Solipsism is the philosophy that the only thing you can really be sure to exist is your own mind, but the word is also used to describe the sentiment that one's own perspective is the *only* perspective. Non-white people face a racialized form of solipsism – the idea that the norms, views, practices, etc. standard in white cultures are the only ones that are acceptable – or that exist at all – *a lot*.

For example, my mother, a former child therapist, used to work at a center that served youths whose families had been mandated to receive therapy. Such parents cannot choose to refuse therapeutic services without serious consequences, and there are grave penalties for parents who do not comply with the process. One day, a toddler African American boy walked into the center with his mother, passing my mother and her colleagues – all of whom were white – as the group headed to a staff meeting.

"Well," one of my mother's coworkers said, "we already know what's wrong with *him*."

"We *do*?" my mom asked, baffled when everyone else nodded.

"It's *obvious*," someone else said.

"It *is*?" my mother asked, utterly perplexed.

"She had that baby boy's hair in pigtails," her colleague explained. "That dysfunctional woman wanted a daughter instead of a son and is treating him as though he were a girl."

"*No*," my mother explained. "That mother put her son's hair in pigtails so that his afro will be fluffier when she unbraids his hair. And in African American culture, particularly among lower socio-economic classes, pigtails are a gender-neutral hairstyle for little kids."

This is both a funny anecdote *and* a horrifying tale – if my mother hadn't been there, her colleagues may have insisted that the boy's mother was trying to force her tiny son to be identified as a girl, and her honest protests that she wasn't could have been treated as noncompliance to tragic ends. Fortunately, my mother's colleagues received her insight constructively and rejected the notion that the little boy's mother was exhibiting pathological behavior.

In two sentences, my mother punctured solipsism at her workplace, awakening her coworkers to the reality that white gender norms cannot be taken for granted as the only gender norms that exist. Sometimes you don't need to have a full-blown "discussion" about race. Sometimes, you simply need to remind the people around you that the perspectives, experiences, mores, etc. of their own race aren't universal.

For example:

DERMATOLOGY PROFESSOR: We need to supplement the textbooks we're using.

DERMATOLOGY DEPARTMENT FACULTY CHAIR: Why? These are the standard dermatology textbooks.

DERMATOLOGY PROFESSOR: Look.... [Flips through textbooks.] These textbooks don't have pictures of afflicted non-white skin. Skin conditions commonly look different on white people and people of color. If our students don't learn what skin diseases look like on people of different backgrounds, then they'll be unable to diagnose non-white patients. If we use these textbooks, we're producing doctors who are only for white people.

Addressing solipsism is a two-step move. First, point out the solipsism – that the dermatology textbooks don't include pictures that show what skin disorders look like on non-white skin. (This is, in fact, true of *most* diagnostic dermatology textbooks.)[9] Second, if necessary, underline the solipsism's implications. In the above conversation, the solipsism is the unconscious notion that white skin is the only skin on which a dermatologist needs to learn to diagnose disease. And the implications are that white people are the *only* people – or the only ones whose health matters; that if you learn how to treat white people and only white people, you've received a complete medical education; that it's acceptable to deprive entire races of people of potentially life-saving care – that their lives and deaths don't matter. Note that in the conversation above, the professor does not list all the implications I do. Salespeople have a saying: Once the shopper has agreed to buy, shut up. Once you've sold your interlocutor on the wrongfulness of the situation, there's no need to say more. If articulating one sinister implication is enough to get your point across, stop after one. However, because things that are normalized come to seem benign, it may take you listing many unfortunate implications before you get your point across. (Note that the speaker starts from the assumption that the chair *wants* to use the best educational resources as opposed to accusing the chair of racism or of not caring about non-white people, etc. In other words, the speaker does not try to shame the chair, which could be less strategic and counterproductive, but instead provides the chair with a positive action option.)

In situations such as the one I described involving my mother, one could take the second step of describing the unfortunate implications of the faulty thinking by making a comment such as:

> This issue goes beyond hair. It connects to how we respond to the spectrum of ways the families we serve communicate, behave, and discipline. When we take for granted that white ways are everyone's ways – or are the best or only legitimate ways – we process cultural difference as deviance.

If you decide to take the second step, think strategically about where and when to do so. For example, if you are in my mother's position, and your colleagues are reeling from the magnitude of the error they made and the harm it could have caused – and also embarrassed that their junior-most coworker had to bring it to their attention – wait before taking step two so your listeners don't feel you are rubbing salt into a wound and turn defensive. You might raise the issue again at a subsequent staff meeting after people have had time to cool down. You could say that you were thinking more about the episode, cast the blame on psychology departments for not warning against solipsism (thereby graciously letting your colleagues off the hook), and engage your colleagues not as culprits but problem-solvers by inviting them to work with you in mitigating against the professional consequences of psychology programs' failure to teach cultural competence. On the other hand, if your colleagues are *intrigued* by the fact that some little African American boys wear their hair in pigtails and delve into a conversation about cultural difference, go ahead and take step two then and there.

Addressing solipsism can also mean helping someone understand that other people experience the world differently than he or she does; therefore, just because someone's account of his or her experiences is different, unrecognizable, or seemingly implausible, doesn't mean that that account is dishonest, distorted, or otherwise wrong. For example, a white friend admitted to me that when non-whites talk about the prevalence of racism, she often doubts them. I pointed out to a white friend that when she came to visit me from out of town, even though the doorman of my building had never seen her before, he welcomed her into the lobby. In contrast, even though I am a *resident* of the building, the doorman has rudely interrogated me as to my presence there. I explained that I am not asking her to possess the supernatural ability to know that a doorman who is friendly and courteous to her may be rude and racist to me. I *am* asking her to accept that racism has a way of splitting someone into a Dr. Jekyll and Mr. Hyde and that just because she has only interacted with the former does not mean that the latter does not exist. I am saying that conclusions such as "Greg is such a friendly doorman that I can't believe he'd be racist, so Shannon must be mistaken – or lying to get sympathy and attention" or "I've only had positive interactions with the police; therefore, the police are respectful and responsible (apart from a few bad apples) and anyone who says otherwise is wrong" are poor reasoning.

Solipsism can disguise itself as logic or common sense because, in many realms of life, our personal experiences provide reliable information on larger realities. But many people fail to realize how much their personal experiences are *contingent* upon their race and thus think they can extrapolate their experiences to others and disregard accounts of experiences that contradict their own.

The inverse of solipsism is empathy. Antiracists empathize with victims of racism. Effective antiracists also empathize with *racists*. Empathy does not mean *agreeing* that someone else is right to feel as they do – it just means being *capable* of feeling as someone else does. Racists are often unsympathetic to people of other backgrounds and their allies. If you, as an antiracist, are equally unable to understand your adversary's perspective, you and your interlocutor are likely to talk past each other. But, if you can comprehend, you can connect, and if you can make a connection, you can often make a change.

For example, suppose at a Parent Teacher Association meeting, a white parent says:

> I'm tired of the school constantly focusing on racial sensitivity. Kids need to toughen up and not be so easily offended. I expect my child to have the grit to get through the day without being coddled, and children of color should do so, too.

You may have several – legitimate – reactions to a comment such as this. You may feel that someone who believes that prejudice is not something to be eradicated but endured is a reprobate. You may think the parent is an idiot if he or she can't distinguish *racism* from other challenges of childhood from earning a poor grade or getting cut from the soccer team. You may wonder what sort of churl thinks treating someone with basic decency is coddling him or her. You may conclude, *This person is a racist*. All these are perfectly justifiable reactions.

But a justifiable reaction is not necessarily the same as an effective *response*.

There's a saying that no one thinks he's a villain. Similarly, very few people think they are racists. So, if you call someone a racist – even for the good reason that she or he *is* one – the person may become too enflamed to heed you. Your interlocutor is likely to be distracted from the situation at hand by what he or she sees as the most pressing issue – what from his or her perspective is your wild, unjust, and impugning mischaracterization.

Empathy in this context might mean recognizing that to someone who's never been the target of racism, racism may not seem like a life-threatening and life-ruining form of oppression but an inconvenience or annoyance – or delusion. When such a parent says that he or she believes children of color should, like her child, be expected to deal with difficult issues and carry on, the parent might, in his or her solipsism, be unaware that the children of color he or she is holding to the same standard as his or her child are not reckoning with the same *challenges*, but rather more and weightier ones.

From this realization, you can focus your response not on the immorality or idiocy of the parent but on noting why the parent's opinion can *seem* reasonable and explaining why, because of the mammoth difference in grit required of otherwise similarly situated white and non-white children, it is, in fact, *not*. You could respond as follows:

> You: What I hear you saying is that the world is a tough place, and we have to raise our children to be tough if they are to succeed in it. That's absolutely true. But I also hear you saying that your child is expected to have sufficient grit to make it through the day, and we should expect the same of children of color. The problem with that reasoning is that, all other factors held constant, it takes exponentially more grit to get through the day as a non-white child than as a white one.

Yes, your child may have to deal with a teacher who has an unpleasant personality and a bully teasing him about his ears on top of trying to earn good grades in rigorous classes while balancing a host of extracurricular activities. Children of color must deal with all of that, too. But then, they must go to a history class in which the teacher explains that George Washington wasn't a bad person for owning slaves and visiting genocide upon Native Americans – that he was just a man of his time, even though a teacher who made such a comment about a perpetrator who enslaved and committed genocide against white people, such as Hitler, would have placed his job in jeopardy. Our children must deal with a student body president telling a racist joke denigrating the intelligence of people of our race at a school assembly, and the teachers not correcting him but laughing. They're then forced to struggle to respect those teachers as authority figures and trust they are accurately perceiving our children's own intelligence when they grade our kids' essays or decide whether to recommend them for the honors levels of courses next year. Your son has never faced his favorite teacher pulling him aside to give him a holiday gift – a book to which the teacher says your son will *really* be able to relate – only to find that the story has nothing to do with him, his interests, or who he is as a person – that, even though he comes from a middle-class family, the book is about a child of his racial background's struggles with poverty in a dysfunctional ethnic community.[10]

These aren't just the kinds of things that ruin your day – they're the kinds of things that end your *life*. Research suggests that the stress of a force as dehumanizing as racism leads to Black people "weathering" – prematurely aging, suffering worse health outcomes, and dying earlier.[11]

So, for you to say that children of color should just handle the challenges that come to them the way your child does doesn't make sense, because your son doesn't have to handle the challenges ours do. And while there are non-racist arguments for and against "trigger warnings" and "safe spaces," let us not fail to recognize that for white children, the *whole school* is a space safe from racial harassment, so having a safe space isn't about whether non-white children get special treatment – it's about whether they get access to the same level of protection *anywhere* on campus that white students experience *everywhere* on campus. Let's have this conversation realizing that your ability to mock the idea of "trigger warnings" comes not from the fact that your son valiantly deals with racial material that triggers him but from the fact that your son has something far more indulgent than trigger warnings: the luxury of a curriculum that doesn't include any anti-white racism for him to be warned *about*, such as "classic" works of literature that contain denigrating stereotypes of people of his background.

Let's break down this response. Part of what makes the response empathetic is that the speaker agrees where he or she can – the speaker affirms the value of rearing strong and resilient children. If you can frame your response not as "You're wrong" but rather as "You and I share the same premise, but here's where we diverge...," you can draw your listener in instead of shutting him or her off.

Furthermore, by understanding the other person's feelings and looking at the world through his eyes, you can anticipate the parts of your argument that are unconvincing and bolster them. Too often, antiracists talk past people because they make arguments that resonate with *themselves* and expect those arguments to persuade someone whose views are nothing like theirs. For example, consider the example the parent gave about the teacher's defense of George Washington. If you're African American or Native American, it may be obvious to you that Washington was a perpetrator because the atrocities he perpetrated were against your people. However, if you simply say, "My child had to face the indignity of a teacher defending Washington as a man of his era," people from other races, who are used to Washington's valorization, may not understand why that's wildly inappropriate. Empathy alerts you to the fact that you need to analogize – that the white parent may not feel what a person of color feels when someone who enslaved or exterminated his or her ancestors is lionized. The white parents may only understand the other perspective when asked to imagine what the reaction would be if a historical figure who enslaved or committed genocide against people of their own race was similarly exculpated.

Similarly, empathy puts you in the perspective of the white parent who might think, "So, my child gets teased for his big ears, another child gets teased in a racialized way for his big nose – what's the difference?" It makes you realize that you must go beyond making an assertion to make an argument. "Racial harassment is different from other forms of bullying," is an assertion. When you *support* that claim, for example, by explaining "weathering," now you're making an argument. The white parent might still be upset with the idea of racial sensitivity, but she can't refute the difference – that racism, unlike other forms of bullying, has the aforementioned epidemiological impact on an entire population.

Here, you may be thinking, "Sure, the response starts out agreeing with the hostile parent, but it's still zealously oppositional." That's true. But being empathetic is not about declining to make necessary points with sufficiently strong language – it's about not being gratuitously provocative.

Nor does being empathetic mean trying to phrase your remarks so gently that, by the end of your comment, the parent whose comment you're rebutting is nodding in agreement. First, that strategy is unlikely to work. Second, it's not the goal.

Being empathetic doesn't mean that, in the moment, the person to whom you're speaking is going to find your comments agreeable – it means she's going to find them *audible*. The person you're addressing doesn't have to instantly *heed* you – the goal is for her to *hear* you. Your goal, vis-à-vis the hostile parent, is to find just enough common ground upon which to plant a seed – not necessarily to reap an immediate harvest. If you're *heard*, your words can be the basis for conversation, relationship, and even mutual learning over time. But if you're too attached to totally changing your listener(s) in one conversation, you may talk too long, without enough empathy, without any back-and-forth, etc. – and that will get you *tuned out*.

And even if you never win over that parent, when a racial discussion takes place in a public arena such as a Parent Teacher Association (PTA) meeting, every other person in the room is like a potential juror whom you have the opportunity to sway. When the hostile parent spoke up, there were likely others in the room who thought to themselves, "She may not have expressed herself in the nicest way, but I think she has a point." Even if you don't reach the parent who made the comment, you can still persuade others who agree with her or who haven't yet made up their minds.

In contrast, if at the meeting you stand up and simply say, "Only a bigot or an ignoramus would oppose being racially sensitive to schoolchildren," you won't have said anything inaccurate, but you *will* have committed a serious strategic blunder.

It won't seem like it at first. You'll probably get some cheers and claps. Others might follow your lead and condemn racial insensitivity as well. No one else might dare to take to the podium and criticize racial sensitivity the rest of the night. In fact, as you participate in the school community for the next few months, you might never hear racial sensitivity attacked *again*. It will seem that the issue is settled – that the antiracists *won*... until next semester when it's announced that the planned anti-bias training for students, faculty, and staff has been canceled because the school board passed a resolution banning such training for promoting the "myth" of white privilege and for being racist to white students.

When you speak empathetically, it allows people the confidence to articulate their opposition to your position. Yes, it's terrible when someone stands up and says schoolchildren don't deserve racial sensitivity. But it's worse when they feel that way and *keep that idea to themselves*, and keep silent during the meeting, and, later, gather with likeminded friends to approach a school administrator or the school board to thwart you.

When antiracists speak in a way that doesn't shame others into self-censoring, they can challenge racist ideas instead of allowing them to fester and flourish in an echo chamber later. Furthermore, they can better gauge what their community *actually* thinks and, thus, develop a more informed and strategic response instead of being lulled into a false sense of complacency.

Beyond being empathetic, the example comment is brief. It takes little over three minutes to say. At a PTA meeting, town hall, or similar forum in which each speaker might be given a few minutes to opine, it's short enough to fit into the allotted time. Remember, your job isn't to give a TED (Technology, Entertainment and Design) talk or defend a dissertation. There are always more examples you could give or references you could cite. The point isn't to say *everything*; it's to say the essential things. It doesn't matter how great an argument you're making is if your audience has drifted off.

Another tactic you can use when discussing or debating race is Historicizing. For example, consider the criticism often levied against affirmative action that it supposedly unfairly advances non-whites – even though its primary beneficiaries are white women[12] and even though a vast array of initiatives past and present, both categorized as affirmative action and not, advance whites.[13]

For example, David Luban, a Georgetown Law Professor, notes that Nazi Bernhard Lösener complained, "There was misadministration in Germany because a large part of the civil service was staffed by people who apparently got their positions not because of their abilities, but because of their ties with Jews." Luban observes: "His comment about civil servants getting their jobs through Jewish connections was a commonplace of the anti-Weimar Republic right, not uniquely Nazi – something more akin to resentment-memes against affirmative action in contemporary U.S. politics."[14]

Similarly, Columbia Law School and UCLA School of Law professor Kimberlé Williams Crenshaw cited historical examples and explained the rationale behind the thinking of Lösener's analogues in a debate:

> It's important to recognize in this context [of discussing the merits of affirmative action] that every significant program that has ever been introduced to assist African-Americans to actually achieve freedom and equality has been denounced as a preference, from the Emancipation Proclamation, which was seen as giving them a preference, giving them something that they didn't deserve, which was basically the value of their labor; to anti-discrimination law that would protect them in their rights to, um, access to hotels and theaters, was seen as special treatment; to even the argument against segregation, which was seen as a preference. So, the point of the matter is, we have to always see these against the base line in society. If we consider the base line to be unfair, if we see the normal status quo as discriminatory, then these interventions are not seen as preferences, they're seen as equal opportunity. If, by contrast, we see society is basically benign, or we think it's OK that there are these deep structural differences that won't go away by ignoring it, but we think that's perfectly acceptable, then we'll understand these interventions as being preferential. I happen to be on the former side of the case. I think having structured inequality over centuries is inconsistent with the deepest values of America, and therefore any kind of intervention that is intending to try to bring about real equality is not preferential, it's in the deepest traditions of equality.[15]

Historicizing allows your interlocutor to recognize that perspectives have precedents. And highlighting the throughline that connects analogous beliefs across time and place gives your interlocutor a new lens through which to evaluate and reevaluate his own view. Here, Crenshaw notes what slaveholders and segregationists had in common with each other – and with some who oppose affirmative action: a belief that because the starting line was equal for everyone, adjusting it forward for Blacks was a cheat, rather than recognizing that because whites had already been given a head start, adjusting the starting line forward for Blacks was a corrective. Here, you can provide a moral of the (his)story – if we accept, for example, that the Emancipation Proclamation and anti-segregation laws were not unjust preferences, then for the argument that affirmative action *is* one to be legitimate, one must first demonstrate that, unlike in the previous eras, the playing field for whites and non-whites is equal. If the playing field is still unequal, then the "unjust preferences" argument is still invalid. (And the inequality of the playing field can be empirically demonstrated as it has been in this book thus far.)

(I note here that just because someone is against affirmative action does not make him or her a racist – however, the "unjust preferences" argument that is either willfully blind or unethically indifferent to structural inequality while arguing that its *mediation* is oppressive *is* a racist argument.)

Sometimes, when discussing or debating race, you don't need to argue or explain but rather to invite introspection by asking the right question. For example, although ninety-three percent of the protests that occurred in the wake of George Floyd's death were peaceful and some of the violence that *did* occur was attributable to *counter*-protesters,[16] some of my white loved ones asked why the protesters wouldn't demonstrate peacefully. I put a question to them in return: "What had they done in response to the peaceful protests against racist police violence? What had they done, for example, when National Football League players knelt during the national anthem?"

The answer was "nothing."

They had not called the mayor's office about the need to reform unjust policing practices. They had not asked their city council representatives to raise the issue. They had not written their congresspeople. It took the turmoil resulting from Floyd's death to rouse them from inaction, but until I asked what they had done in response to peaceful protests, they did not recognize that their own indifferent idleness was the reason some protesters had become violent.

An answer someone arrives at to his or her own question is much more powerful than any answer you could give.

Thus, in that situation, I did not have to explain to my friends that they were nonsensically asking, "Why don't the protesters engage in demonstrations of which my own behavior suggests the ineffectiveness? Why don't the protesters engage in demonstrations that animate me only to condemn them as unpatriotic?" Their own answers made them aware of their illogic.

When I engage in a conversation like this with a friend, I may begin and end by speaking to the value of our relationship to me and my appreciation of his or her character. In other words, I make it clear that my issue is with *the issue* – not with the person holding it. I believe my friends are more than the infelicitous ideas they occasionally express and expect them to grow beyond them – and if either of those things proved not to be true, I would discontinue that friendship. There's no rule of thumb for how long you should give someone to grow, but if and when a relationship becomes a source of ongoing distress, it's time to let it go.

Mental health professionals use the term "cognitive distortion" to label certain warped ways of thinking that manifest in the context of mental illnesses such as anxiety and depression. But versions of these cognitive distortions sometimes appear in thinking on race. One such cognitive distortion is all-or-nothing thinking or misperceiving reality as being arranged in perfect dichotomies.[17] An example of how this manifests in the context of racial discourse can be seen in the form of comments that point to the wealth, celebrity, or success of individual luminaries of color as "evidence" that racism is not – or is not very serious of – a problem. The thinking here is that if racism were real or grave, then *no* non-whites would have riches, fame, or power and *all* non-whites would be disadvantaged on every axis relative to all whites.

But consider a Dakota Native American man named Charles A. Eastman who lived from 1858 to 1939. Eastman earned a bachelor's degree from an Ivy League university and a medical degree from Boston University at a time when many white people couldn't even read. Indeed, he was better educated than most white people are *now*.... His medical school education was particularly useful when he was treating the survivors of the Wounded Knee massacre.

Just because a *few* non-whites are better off than *some* whites in *some* ways doesn't mean that racism is not an urgent problem.

When faced with all-or-nothing thinking, offer examples that puncture the dichotomy.

Another reasoning error is belief bias. Belief bias is accepting or rejecting an argument based on one's agreement with that argument's conclusion.[18] In discussions on racism, belief bias often manifests when person A asserts that racial injustice exists and that a particular initiative is part of the solution to it. If person B doesn't like the solution, he or she goes beyond rejecting it to insist that the problem itself – racial injustice – doesn't exist. When faced with belief bias, cite to the empirical evidence supporting your underlying argument. For example, "Councilman, you can disagree that reallocating some of the funding that currently goes to the police for non-crime-related activities to other professionals should be part of police reform, but I don't believe you can argue against the problem of racist police violence that this solution seeks to address. It is a fact that unarmed Black men are about four times more likely than unarmed white men to be shot by the police."[19]

Motive attribution asymmetry is another cognitive bias you're likely to encounter. It is the tendency to believe that those on your side are motivated by ingroup love, while your opponents are motivated by outgroup hate.[20] Many people, for example, believe that those who argue that some of the non-crime-related responsibilities and concomitant funding currently allocated to the police should be diverted to other professionals are motivated by a hatred of the police. An antiracist needs to be aware that his or her motives are likely to be misattributed and underline that his or her positions are not animated by a hatred of the police or of white people, etc. but out of a concern for the safety and dignity of non-whites. Thus, an antiracist might say:

> I have a friend whose adult son is a man of color with schizophrenia. He is not a criminal, but he *is* sick, and he sometimes suffers mental health crises during which, with neither malice nor intent, he becomes a danger those around him. When I say we should defund the police, I'm not saying, 'Defund the police because every police officer is evil; thus, the force doesn't deserve taxpayer support.' I'm saying that it is as cruelly unfair to expect the police to handle mental health crises as it would be to expect psychologists and psychiatrists to apprehend burglars. I'm saying that when my friend's son needs help, the responsibility for aiding him – and the funding that pays those who do so – should belong to the mental health professionals equipped to handle the situation and not to the police.

Racists often intuit the concept of motive attribution asymmetry even if they don't know the formal term for it. However, they incorrectly perceive *themselves* as victims whose motives are being misattributed because they don't recognize their racist beliefs as hatred. Therefore, racists often reflexively profess outgroup love when they make racist statements – a rhetorical move that commonly (and notoriously) takes the form of the claim that "some of my best friends are Black."

This discursive technique has a long provenance. For example, consider how pro-slavery writer Edward A. Pollard wrote about Blacks in 1859:

> I love the simple and unadulterated slave, with his geniality, his mirth, his swagger, and his nonsense; I love to look upon his countenance, shining with content and grease; I love to study his affectionate heart; I love to mark that peculiarity in him, which beneath all his buffoonery, exhibits him as a creature of the tenderest sensibilities, mingling his joys and his sorrows with those of his master's home.... But the "genteel" slave, who is inoculated with white notions, affects superiority, and exchanges his simple and humble ignorance for insolate airs, is altogether another creature, and my especial abomination.[21]

Pollard presages the "I'm not a racist – some of my best friends are Black, but..." formula perfectly. He tries to pre-empt being accused of bigotry for considering it abominable for Black people to consider themselves equal to whites by first stating how very much he loves Blacks.

In my experience, those who use the phrase "some of my best friends are Middle Eastern/Asian/Black/Latino/Native American" are almost always unwittingly lying to themselves as well as to you. (Less than ten percent of whites *actually* have Black best friends.)[22] They haven't given any meaningful thought as to whether the specters they're invoking are indeed their "best" friends or are even truly their friends at all as opposed to casual acquaintances. They're also caught in an all-or-nothing cognitive distortion, in the grip of which they believe that one who has positive feelings about individuals of a certain race therefore cannot also have prejudices against that race as a whole.

In other words, the "some of my best friends" defense, while illegitimate, is often deployed in good faith. Thus, because the speaker is wielding it sincerely, until you break through this defense, you may find it difficult for any of your points to penetrate. He or she thinks, "Because some of my best friends are green, my attitudes toward green people cannot be in need of correction; therefore, I can disregard what this person is saying to me." Furthermore, the foundation for such faulty reasoning can seem unimpeachable: "I am the authority on my own experience – who is someone else to tell me what color my best friends are?"

However, because so much of a person's unwillingness to reevaluate their racial attitudes can hinge on their self-perception as someone with close, deep relationships to green people, if you can point out the holes in this defense, you can often journey through them to reach the person.

So, how do you do that?

First, you can point to data to help the person with whom you're speaking recognize the subconscious cynicism with which the phrase is deployed. You can note that Duke sociology Professor and former President of the American Sociological Association Eduardo Bonilla-Silva found that while "whites used this phrase to inflate their associations with blacks and, occasionally, to be able to say something very negative about blacks, blacks did not resort to similar phrases to state their views about whites."[23]

Second, you can share Bonilla-Silva's findings about the nature of whites' "friendships" with Blacks and use it to help your interlocutor evaluate their own friendships with green people. What Bonilla-Silva found was that:

> superficial contacts (for college students, sports, music, and the occasional friendly talk with a black student and, [for adults who were not in college], the occasional lunch or talk at work with blacks) are used as self-evident facts of friendship. Missing from these reports of friendships with blacks is evidence of trust, of the capacity of confiding, and

of interactions with these friends beyond the place or situation of formal contact (classroom, assigned roommates, or job). Finally, these "friendships" with blacks always disappear after the reason for the formal interaction ends – taking a class, rooming, playing in a band or in a sports team, or working in the same company.[24]

So, you can invite the person with whom you're speaking to open his or her planner and review the appointments from the previous month – how many social engagements were with green people? You can inquire about the person's most recent major life event gathering such as his or her bachelor/bachelorette party, baby shower, or parent's or grandparent's funeral – ask how many of the attendees were green. When was the last time they talked to these "best friends" and how often do they do so?

People of whom you ask such questions are often shocked to find that, in fact, *none* of their best friends are green. And the realization that they were wrong about the role that race plays in their own relationships can open them to the notion that they might be wrong about race in other domains of life, too.

Last technique: Sometimes, when discussing race, you will encounter someone unwittingly affirming dissonant values. When that happens, point out the contradiction. For example, consider the statement, "In my classroom, I teach that George Washington was a hero because he helped found a nation based on the principles of 'life, liberty, and the pursuit of happiness' articulated in the Declaration of Independence." Here, you can point out the contradiction in believing that life, liberty, and the pursuit of happiness are values both so important that founding a nation ostensibly based on them renders one a hero, yet so trivial that it is not villainous to deny them to entire races of people.

When learning to waltz, there are basic steps that one masters. Everything you see on the ballroom floor is but an elaboration upon them. Similarly, once you learn the underlying rhetorical forms you'll encounter and wield again and again in discussions on race and racism, you're equipped to speak powerfully and persuasively about race no matter the context.

Notes

1. Brad N. Greenwood, Rachel R. Hardeman, Laura Huang, and Aaron Sojourner, "Physician–Patient Racial Concordance and Disparities in Birthing Mortality for Newborns," *Proceedings of the National Academy of Sciences* 117, no. 35 (September 2020): 21195, https://doi.org/10.1073/pnas.1913405117.
2. Penn Medicine, "Minority Students Still Underrepresented in Medical Schools," September 4, 2019, https://www.pennmedicine.org/news/news-releases/2019/september/minority-students-still-underrepresented-in-medical-schools.
3. Dana Goldstein and Jugal K. Patel, "Need Extra Time on Tests? It Helps to Have Cash," *New York Times,* July 30, 2019, https://www.nytimes.com/2019/07/30/us/extra-time-504-sat-act.html.
4. Ibid.

5 "Nonwhite School Districts Get $23 Billion Less Than White Districts Serving the Same Number of Students," EdBuild, February 25, 2021, https://edbuild.org/content/23-billion.
6 Sophie Quinton and National Journal, "The Race Gap in High School Honors Classes," *The Atlantic*, December 11, 2014, https://www.theatlantic.com/politics/archive/2014/12/the-race-gap-in-high-school-honors-classes/431751/.
7 Monica Rhor, "Woman's Story Shows How Systems Are Failing Black Girls," *USA Today*, May 15, 2019, https://www.usatoday.com/in-depth/news/nation/2019/05/13/racism-black-girls-school-discipline-juvenile-court-system-child-abuse-incarceration/3434742002/.
8 Ibid.
9 Roni Caryn Rabin, "Dermatology Has a Problem with Skin Color," *New York Times*, August 30, 2020, https://www.nytimes.com/2020/08/30/health/skin-diseases-black-hispanic.html.
10 These examples are all derived from just a few of my sister's and my school experiences.
11 O. Kenrik Duru, Nina T. Harawa, Dulcie Kermah, and K.C. Norris, "Allostatic Load Burden and Racial Disparities in Mortality," *Journal of the National Medical Association* 104, nos. 1–2 (2012): 89–95, https://doi.org/10.1016/s0027-9684(15)30120-6.
12 Sally Kohn, "Affirmative Action Has Helped White Women More Than Anyone," *Time*, June 17, 2013, https://ideas.time.com/2013/06/17/affirmative-action-has-helped-white-women-more-than-anyone/.
13 See for example, Ira Katznelson, *When Affirmative Action Was White: An Untold History of Racial Inequality in Twentieth-Century America* (New York: W.W. Norton & Company, 2005); Catholic Charities USA, *Poverty and Racism: Overlapping Threats to the Common Good* (Alexandria, VA: Catholic Charities USA, 2008), https://www.catholiccharitiesusa.org/wp-content/uploads/2018/04/Policy-Paper-Poverty-and-Racism-1.pdf; Camille G. Caldera, "Legacy, Athlete, and Donor Preferences Disproportionately Benefit White Applicants, per Analysis," *The Harvard Crimson*, October 23, 2019, https://www.thecrimson.com/article/2019/10/23/nber-admissions-data/.
14 David Luban, "Complicity and Lesser Evils: A Tale of Two Lawyers" (paper, International Nuremberg Principles Academy, Nuremberg, Germany, September 27–28, 2019).
15 "Transcript," It's Time to End Affirmative Action, Intelligence Squared Debates, October 8, 2020, https://www.intelligencesquaredus.org/debates/its-time-end-affirmative-action.
16 "Demonstrations & Political Violence in America: New Data for Summer 2020," ACLED, last modified September 3, 2020, https://acleddata.com/2020/09/03/demonstrations-political-violence-in-america-new-data-for-summer-2020/.
17 Rob Wilson and Rhena Branch, *Cognitive Behavioral Therapy for Dummies* (Chichester: John Wiley & Sons, Ltd., 2009), 21.
18 Jacqueline P. Leighton, "The Assessment of Logical Reasoning," in *The Nature of Reasoning*, eds. Robert J. Sternberg and Jacqueline P. Leighton (Cambridge: Cambridge University Press, 2004), 300.
19 Joe Fox, Adrian Blanco, Jennifer Jenkins, Julie Tate, and Wesley Lowery, "What We've Learned about Police Shootings 5 Years after Ferguson," *The Washington Post*, August 9, 2019, https://www.washingtonpost.com/nation/2019/08/09/what-weve-learned-about-police-shootings-years-after-ferguson/?arc404=true.

20 Adam Waytz, Liane L. Young, and Jeremy Ginges, "Motive Attribution Asymmetry for Love vs. Hate Drives Intractable Conflict," *Proceedings of the National Academy of Sciences* 111, no. 44 (November 2014): 15687–15692, https://doi.org/10.1073/pnas.1414146111.
21 Edward A. Pollard, *Black Diamonds Gathered in the Darkey Homes of the South* (New York: Pudney & Russell Publishers, 1859), 57–58, HathiTrust.
22 Eduardo Bonilla-Silva, *Racism Without Racists: Colorblind Racism and the Persistence of Racial Inequality in the United States* (Lanham, MD: Rowman & Littlefield, 2018), 11.
23 Ibid., 166.
24 Ibid., 111.

Chapter 3

Unweaving systemic racism

In the wake of George Floyd's killing, corporation after corporation made pro-racial justice statements. Our television sets, computer screens, and smartphones blared and glowed with disavowals and promises, condemnations and affirmations, confessions of past wrongs and New Year's Eve-worthy declarations of intent to do better.

But do you know how many of the corporations that decided to take responsive action actually made substantive changes?

One in ten.[1]

Your own community or institution may also have struggled to navigate from an awkward and pressured sense of obligation to *say* something to figuring out how to *do* anything – much less something that made a real difference. The failure of almost *all* the companies that intended to do something meaningful to follow through shows that when it comes to racial justice, Martin Luther King may have had a dream, but you need a *plan* because, ultimately, high-minded visions are achieved via something deceptively mundane: systems.

To unweave institutional racism, organizations and communities need systems that change *who* they are and *how* they are. What do I mean by that? In Chapter 1, I described how, controlling for socio-economics, non-whites are less likely to be given mortgage loans than whites.[2] And, per a U.S. governmental report, banks' boards of directors and senior employees are not diverse.[3] Suppose you wanted to work to fix that, starting with one bank. You would need to change *who* the bank is by transforming it into a more multiracial body of people. But you would also need to change *how* the bank is by putting policies in place that ensure equitable lending practices.

If you want to move your organization or community toward a real change but do not have a leadership role, reach out to the appropriate person and, depending on what you feel would be more persuasive, make either a *business case* or a *values case* for racial justice.

Making a business case may sound like this:

YOU: I'd like to talk to you about some research I've done on how being strategic about recruiting and retaining talent can significantly improve our profits.

DOI: 10.4324/9781003144298-4

YOUR SUPERIOR: I'm all ears.
YOU: The consulting firm McKinsey found that when led by ethnically and culturally diverse executive teams, companies were thirty-three to thirty-five percent more likely to achieve above-average profits. And when those companies had ethnically and culturally diverse boards of directors, they were *forty-three percent* more likely.[4] There is a meaningful, positive connection between a company's diversity and its bottom line, so I think we should put some systems in place to foster greater diversity in *our* organization.

From that point, you can pivot to suggesting your organization employ the ideas in this chapter.

A values case for racial justice can sound like this:

YOU: I've been thinking about our equestrian society's stated values of responsibility for our horses and for each other and of respect for all members of our community human and equine. I've always been proud to be part of an organization that emphasizes character and inspired to reflect upon what those qualities look like in practice. Lately, I've been considering what responsibility and respect mean in regard to racial justice.
LEADER: What do you mean?
YOU: Well, I know our intention is to respect people regardless of color, and yet the upper ranks of our leadership are disproportionately white. I don't think any of us believe that equestrian talent is inequitably distributed, so that suggests that, somehow, what we *do* in regard to recruitment and retention of members and promoting them to greater heights isn't reflecting the respect we *feel* for all people and the gifts they have to offer. Furthermore, I've witnessed equestrians of color being mistaken for stable hands and not infrequently heard respected trainers make racist jokes. Whether or not this behavior is intentional, out of *respect* for our fellow horsemen and women, we're *responsible* for putting systems in place to make sure people are treated with fairness and dignity.

Another way to initiate the process of change is by having a conversation about color in the course of your normal duties – if you recruit, manage, or serve people – if your job or role has an impact on other human beings at all – then race is relevant to your work. Use your organization's recruitment process to talk about diversifying your personnel. When you and other faculty members are asked to recommend kids for specialized programs, bring up the study that found that "a high-achieving white student is twice as likely as an equally high-achieving black student to get assigned to [a gifted students] program."[5] Then, once you've opened the door to discussions of racial justice, suggest your organization or community look more broadly at issues of diversity, equity, and inclusion.

As these strategies show, you can single-handedly push your organization or community toward racial justice. But just because you *can* make change unilaterally doesn't necessarily mean you *must*. You can reach out to people of color and people of character in your organization or community whom you know are – or think might be – interested in racial justice and invite them to meet to discuss the problems or potential solutions. Then, *on behalf of the group*, approach senior leadership to let them know that a significant number of their people are invested in increasing diversity, equity, and inclusion. Attorneys and staff of color and our allies at my law firm used this method to encourage leadership to make our firm's commitment to social justice even more robust in the wake of George Floyd's killing.

Let's talk about the changes organizations and communities need to make to *who* they are first. Some entities outsource the task of figuring this out to diversity, equity, and inclusion consulting firms, which can be wonderful resources. But if an outside vendor is outside the budget, don't let the fact that you can't afford to do one *particular* thing convince you that you're unable to do *anything*. As with renovating a house, with some know-how, conducting a racial justice audit of your organization or community's population can be a do-it-yourself project.

One component of racial justice auditing is gathering qualitative data – invite people in your organization or community to share their experiences with race and racism there. Wondering what to say? No need – your job is to *listen*.

As a person of color who's spent a lifetime helping the predominantly white institutions of which I've been a part become more diverse, inclusive, and equitable – from my southern, private, college preparatory alma mater to the transatlantic law firm where I work – I'm a veteran of racial justice listening sessions. Here are the best practices:

First, if you are acting with institutional support, have the senior-most leader available hold the conversations. Doing so signals how seriously your organization or community takes racial justice, and that sincerity will call forth more profound, candid, useful responses. Furthermore, it maximizes the discussions' efficiency and effectiveness if the person holding them is someone with the power to act in response. You can coach a senior person toward such a discussion by helping her understand that her listening is as powerful as her voice and that there are people in the organization or community who *want* higher ups to exercise their leadership in the realm of racial issues. If you know that the leader values diversity, equity, and inclusion, inform him of the value of demonstrating that through such an initiative and apprise him of the resulting capital he will accrue.

Second, ask for participation via email, flyer, by public announcement, or through a similarly indirect manner. This allows invitees to mull your request – or even decline it – less awkwardly than in person, one-on-one. Simply state that you are looking to make the organization or community more diverse, inclusive, and equitable and, to that end, are inviting community members to share their experiences.

Third, if you are an employer, hold the conversations during normal work hours. When you ask your employees to advise you on how you can improve your business, they're performing labor that should be compensated at the rate of any other task they might be asked to do. Yes, trying to make the workplace more racially just is for employees' benefit (though hardly exclusively)[6] – but so would repainting the lunchroom… and you wouldn't ask them to stay late and do *that* for free.

Fourth, extend the invitation to as many people as possible – as is always true of data science, the larger the sample size, the more representative the information gathered.

Fifth, make sure the logistics of the conversation are conducive to open and candid talk. The discussions should either be held one-on-one in a private space or in a group session facilitated by an outside moderator. At least an hour should be allotted for a one-on-one discussion and two and a half hours for a group discussion, so there's time enough to go deep.

These dialogues will provide you with valuable qualitative data. To give one example, when, in the wake of George Floyd's death, one of the co-deputy chairs of my firm held listening sessions with all the Black associates, she was shocked when I told her how Black and Asian women attorneys at the firm (including me) were commonly initially mistaken for secretaries by colleagues. Shortly after, she planned a diversity, equity, and inclusion training that addressed racial stereotyping. Other issues you might learn of include lack of diversity, inadvertently exclusionary practices, bias in mentoring, inequitable distribution of opportunity, uneven playing fields, and devaluing of racial justice efforts. Or those problems may become visible to you when you begin incorporating quantitative data into your racial audit. Either way, as this chapter continues, I'll explain how both numbers and narratives can show us what we need to remedy and offer step-by-step guides to fixing the issues you find.

In the paragraph above, I described how listening sessions were conducted with Black associates. I've also attended group listening sessions only for people of color but not just for any one minority race as well as those open to all races. If you seek to learn the experiences of one particular group, then the listening sessions can be conducted with people of just that culture. If you hope to gain insight into the experiences of people of color in general, then you can hold sessions that include folks of multiple minority groups. If the goal is to allow people of all backgrounds not just to articulate their experiences and thoughts but to hear *each other*, then listening sessions should involve both non-whites and whites. Bear in mind, though, that the less demographic affinity people have with each other, the more people might be likely to self-censure – and this is true not just in the racial context but also in the context of gender and other forms of identity. This can be mitigated through the use of one-on-one listening sessions or by hosting a mix of group listening sessions – some for a single race of color, some for people of color of any race, and some for any race of people at all – and by inviting people to participate as they choose, including in more than one type of conversation.

"The simple recipe for managing diversity…" according to scholars Elizabeth Hirsh and Donald Tomaskovic-Devey "is to develop metrics, make them transparent, and hold people accountable, just like for any other outcome of interest, be it profit, sales, or market penetration."[7] So, take account of the racial demographics of your organization or community. For example, a company would gather the numbers on the races of personnel by tier and department as well as of its board. Ask: Are the demographics reflective of the larger community or – in the case of companies that recruit nationally or internationally – the larger society? (No cheating by, for example, comparing your organization's demographics to that of the disproportionately white, suburban town in which it's located instead of those of the larger metropolis or county, given the role of institutional racism in carving out those de facto segregated white enclaves in the first place.)[8] Does the organization get whiter as you move up the hierarchy? Are people of color – or peoples of certain colors – concentrated in a specific area?

Even if people of color are present in your organization or community, when you disaggregate and scrutinize the demographic data, you may discover that though your entity is as colorful as a rainbow, it's as stratified as one, too. For example, a company may find that it hires plenty of green people – but almost all of them as janitors. A school may discover that it only hires orange people to teach Orangelish language classes – never math, science, or history. An organization may pride itself on the number of women who hold leadership roles without realizing that they're almost all white – that the women at the institution work in the same place but in two different eras… for the women of color, it might as well be a century earlier.

Sometimes entities struggle to diversify because non-whites aren't present in an arena in numbers that approximate their proportion of the population (for example, white people are seventy-six percent of the U.S. population,[9] but eighty-eight percent of its lawyers,[10] which means that people of color are underrepresented among attorneys). But that's not an excuse – it's a call to action. For example, a law firm might donate to and incentivize its attorneys to serve as mentors and volunteers at an organization such as the Pipeline to Practice Foundation which offers "programming, coaching and mentorship for diverse law students."[11] Or a ballet company might undertake an initiative such as Project Plié which identifies and trains ballet students from underrepresented demographics.[12] (By the way have you looked into how you can get involved with such organizations in your field on an individual level?)

Or intervene even earlier. Think about the tradition of Career Day in which parents visit their children's classrooms to discuss their jobs. In some schools, parents talk about being computer engineers, animators, and botanists –

about careers they *chose*. In others, parents discuss jobs that, while honest and honorable, are those people typically end up in due to *lack* of choice such as grocery store clerk, cleaner, and warehouse worker. And those people are disproportionately non-white.[13]

We ask children what they want to be when they grow up, but children in those latter classrooms can't answer with careers about which they've never heard. We ask them where they want to go in life, ignoring that they don't know anyone who can offer them directions. At Yale Law School, the Black Law Students Association hosted a yearly event called Law School for a Day during which we gave New Haven public school students, predominantly Black and Hispanic, and commonly underprivileged, exactly that. You individually, your peers, or your organization or community could invite students from schools of color to your own place of work or professional school – or falconry club or gymnastics program. Or you could contact school administrators and ask if you and your colleagues could address their students. If an organization sent a half dozen employees or community members each to speak to a different school assembly just twice a year, how many thousands of students might be reached? Or could your office offer a diversity internship to a student? Could your robotics program offer a diversity scholarship to a child? Could you spare a half hour a week to give piano lessons to a youth who would otherwise not have access? Might you invite your peers – or competitors – to do the same?

Many people participate in the Angel Tree tradition during the holidays in which organizations collect impoverished children's holiday gift wishes and volunteer "angels" purchase the toys and clothes so kids who would otherwise find no presents under the Christmas tree can have the joy of unwrapping a gift. But what if there were a tradition of Opportunity Trees? What if an entire office or congregation or fraternal or sororal organization coordinated with racial justice organizations, schools of color, or houses of worship with non-white parishioners to invite teenagers – or upwardly mobile adults – to submit opportunity wishes. For example, one could wish for tutoring in a specific subject or for help preparing for a college entrance exam or writing one's college application or learning English or for an internship in a particular field, and angels could each select a wish to make come true. The more wishes granted, the more orthodontists, firefighters, and astronauts of color we'd have in the long run.

That said, don't default to the excuse that you can't diversify your organization or community because there just aren't enough purple zookeepers. Too often, whether we're looking for a person of color to wear a judge's robe or a tutu, we simply toss up our hands and wail, "I can't find any," as haplessly as a third grader swearing his inability to locate a clean shirt in his messy room. Like the third grader, you probably *can* find that for which you're looking. You probably just need to look more carefully.

Here's how:

If your organization is a company, examine how it hires. Do applicants learn about jobs by reading postings, being recruited, or through word of mouth? As the U.S. Equal Employment Opportunity Commissioner notes:

> While word-of-mouth recruiting in a racially diverse workforce can be an effective way to promote diversity, the same method of recruiting in a non-diverse workforce is a barrier to equal employment opportunity if it does not create applicant pools that reflect the diversity in the qualified labor market (citation omitted).[14]

So, where do you find talented people beyond word of mouth? Make it a practice to recruit for jobs at Historically Black Colleges and Universities, Hispanic-Serving Institutions, Tribal Colleges and Universities (or their non-American equivalents) and, when recruiting from predominantly white schools, at ethnic student affinity groups such as Middle Eastern and North African Law Students Associations or Latino Medical Student Associations. Alert ethnic affinity groups for professionals in your field such as Association of Black Women Historians or the Native American Journalists Association about job openings as well. If you're using a recruiter, tell him or her that you want to see racial variety in the applicants.

What about outside the employment context? Just like many employers, the private, predominantly white, college preparatory school I attended relied on word of mouth to fill admission spaces during my tenure there. (And, at least as of a few years ago, it reserved eighty percent of prekindergarten and kindergarten admission spots for legacies, an affirmative action policy entrenching the racial hierarchy that serves as a grandfather clause to keep the school white.) But many of our peer schools actively seek racial diversity, for example, partnering with organizations such as Prep for Prep, which identifies talented children of color in humble schools and puts them through an intense course of study before placing them in some of the most elite schools in the country (and offering them support and enrichment opportunities through college and beyond). It's simple: If you claim to value diversity, then, when it comes to communities of color, don't be a secret and don't be a stranger.

Want your house of worship to be more diverse? Get creative. Churches sometimes partner with congregations of different racial backgrounds to arrange pulpit and choir swaps.[15] Why not go further and continue swapping on an ongoing basis? Encourage members to make a habit of attending and making tithes, offerings, or other donations to the partner house of worship. Co-host events and initiatives and invite worshippers to use and volunteer in the resources of both places, i.e. the theology classes, premarital counseling, nursery school – and, ultimately, to consider themselves as belonging to both.

Want your dance studio to be more diverse? Ballet teacher and studio owner Cynthia Bradley discovered her student Misty Copeland, who would become the first Black principal ballerina at American Ballet Theater, by temporarily teaching a ballet class at a Boys and Girls Club to scout for talented children of color.[16]

If you want more people of color in your organization or community, *then search in the places where they are.*

Here, you might be thinking, "But I search in the places where everyone is. I can understand what's wrong with word-of-mouth recruiting, but shouldn't, for example, an advertisement placed in a race-neutral venue suffice?"

Here's why it doesn't.

First, what *is* a race-neutral venue? Are you advertising your university, junior orchestra, or teen STEM program online? One in five Native Americans between the ages of three and eighteen don't have home internet access.[17] In the pages of my alumni magazines from Dartmouth, Harvard, and Yale, I often find ads for private elementary and secondary schools and academic programs. But Blacks and Hispanics are underrepresented at America's top 100 colleges – in fact, Blacks are fifteen percent of college-aged Americans, but only nine percent of Ivy League freshman,[18] so when private schools and academic programs advertise in the pages of elite alumni magazines, they aren't taking a race-neutral action – they're extending the invitation to join their schools to a disproportionately low amount of Black and Hispanic families. In a world of continued racial disparities, venues aren't necessarily as race neutral as they appear.

Okay, you think, *but I advertised for a contortionist on the webpage and in the monthly magazine of the primary professional organization of contortionists – what's wrong with that?*

And the answer is: Nothing. That action isn't *wrong* – it's just not *enough*. Martin Luther King, Jr. said in reference to how the government should treat Blacks: "a society that has done something special *against* the Negro for hundreds of years must now do something special *for* him, in order to equip him to compete on a just and equal basis."[19] Similarly, organizations and communities in societies that have done "something special" in terms of hiring bias against Pacific Islanders, Middle Easterners, Asians, Blacks, Native Americans, and Hispanics should make a special effort to pursue such candidates.

Nevertheless, the idea of doing "something special" remains contentious. Though, in an article in *Bloomberg*, Harvard social sciences professor Frank Dobbin observed, "Companies that write affirmative-action plans, which set goals, see more progress toward diversity than companies that don't," many institutions are afraid of quotas and affirmative action. But as the article points out, attempts to increase diversity without them have resulted in a society in which, for example, Black people are 13.4 percent of the U.S. population but only 3.2 percent of those in executive or senior leadership roles.[20]

The theory behind quotas and affirmative action is that the only way to counter the prejudices described in this book – such as the bigotry that causes being Black to make a man a less desirable job applicant than being an ex-convict[21] – is to set targets that approximate what institutional demographics would look like if such racism were lessened. And that theory has data to support it.

For example, although people of color are twenty-four percent of the U.S. population and data does not indicate their underrepresentation in the non-profit world, they're less than twenty percent of nonprofit CEOs and executives despite the fact that whites and non-whites in the nonprofit sector *are equally qualified for leadership roles*.[22] Thus, if quotas and affirmative action were used in the nonprofit sector, it wouldn't demand that less qualified non-whites be chosen over more qualified whites – it would result in qualified non-whites getting the roles they deserved. Conversely, the absence of quotas and affirmative action might be seen as a system of preferences for *whites*, because if non-whites and whites are equally qualified for leadership roles, yet whites are seventy-six percent of the population and eighty percent of nonprofit leaders, then that means qualified non-whites are being passed over for less qualified *whites*.

You can look to both general and specific statistics to get these points across. If diversity and inclusion efforts meant that more qualified whites were being replaced by less qualified people of color, then we would expect more diverse companies to be less profitable. But, as I discussed earlier, more diverse companies are actually significantly *more* profitable, which suggests that diversity and inclusion efforts lessen the practice of companies hiring less qualified whites over more qualified non-whites.[23] This fact also maps onto data showing that diversity increases the creativity of groups as well as the ability to appeal to customers, clients, and investors and offers other benefits.[24] Or you can cite to a specific vivid story: When James D. White, an African American, became the CEO of Jamba Juice, an international juice and smoothie shop, he tripled the diversity of the three highest levels of talent, taking the two highest from twenty to fifty percent... the company's market capitalization increased *five hundred percent*.[25] Under White, diverse professionals were given the opportunity to use their talents – and clearly demonstrated that the opportunity was deserved.

So, what might a good quota look like? *Bloomberg* notes that just months after George Floyd was killed, Estée Lauder promised population parity of Black employees at all levels within the next five years.[26] That's SMART. Remember, as discussed in Chapter 1, racial justice goals need to be Specific, Measurable, Assignable, Realistic, and Time-related. Estée Lauder's plan Specifies a race of people, a quantifiable level of diversity, and at which levels that diversity must be present – all of them. It's Measurable by corporate census; Assignable to Human Resource officers, managers, diversity officers, and/or recruiters; and Realistic and Time-related, containing a feasible yet urgent five-year deadline.

(Estée Lauder explained that in the first five months after making its announcement, it had doubled its rate of Black hiring. By the end of the year, members of the U.S. Executive Leadership Team were to get "diversity dashboards" on their teams. And the company planned to take other steps such as to have all its leaders see to it that there were both internal and external diverse candidates for all jobs at the rank of Executive Director and above before deciding whom to hire, to account for diversity in talent progression and recruitment plans, and to develop a sponsorship and mentorship program for Black employees. These initiatives were complemented by an array of events, trainings, tactics, and acts of transparency. Thus, it seems that Estée Lauder allowed itself five years to reach its goal because it understands that if it is assiduous about sowing the seeds of racial justice in the manner described, five years is when it can expect a harvest. This strategy is congruent with the discussion of approaching the Time-related aspect of SMART goals in Chapter 1 – such goals should be efficient but not so ambitious as to be impracticable).[27]

Implement – or ask for – a policy like that of Estée Lauder at your organization or community. After all, it's important to note that the company's racial justice target wasn't inspired from the top down – it came about in response to employees writing the chairman about their concerns about race in their workplace.[28] You don't have to be in charge to suggest any of the initiatives in this chapter. (But be mindful of contexts in which they are impermissible. For example, as of writing, in California, affirmative action by local and state agencies is banned.)[29] Whether you have a set target or not, though, remember Hirsh and Tomaskovic-Devey's insistence that accountability is key. Someone must be held responsible for making sure the diversity of your organization is, in fact, increasing.

Even if you aren't in charge of or even directly involved with hiring at your company or admission to your community, you still have a role to play. If you're an antiracist, then regardless of your official job title, the *Chief Diversity Officer* is *you*. Take the initiative to make your organization or community less racially homogenous by making non-white organizations and institutions aware of the open positions at your institution and spreading the word among people of color in your personal network.

Next, consider how applications to join your company or community are reviewed. Are applicants required to submit a picture? Do application reviewers come across pictures of candidates while researching them online? Consider that, in 2020, the U.S. Army decided to stop using candidates' photographs in promotion board hearings because it found that when no photographs were used, minorities and women were more likely to be promoted.[30] Thus, though it's counterintuitive, colorblindness – in this context – can help an institution meet a diversity target.

Though it's prudent to research candidates online, you can try to limit the negative impact of knowing an applicant's race. An antiracist system for initial review of applications could look like this: Step one: Neither require nor allow photographs with applications. Step two: Make initial "yes" and "no" piles. Step three: Have a second person research the online presences of those in the "yes" pile and perform a second round of eliminations. This second person must offer a *specific* reason for placing any application in the no pile – no peremptory strikes allowed.

When attorneys picking juries for trials dismiss a potential juror from the jury pool, they must generally give a reason for doing so, and the reason cannot be the juror's race. However, in many such countries, including the United States, attorneys get a certain amount of peremptory strikes – the right to strike jurors without saying why.

You see the problem here, right?[31]

While there may be so many unsuitable candidates in the first round of reviewing applications that it would be inefficient and burdensome to give a reason for every rejection at that point (yet ideal, if possible), from the second review through the extension of offers, disallow peremptory challenges. (And as the hiring process continues, try to prevent letting anyone else see what the candidates look like for as long as possible.)

When the first reviewer gets the applications back, he should then look at the applications in the new "no" pile to see if any merit Batson challenges.

You see, when a lawyer thinks his or her adversary might have stricken a potential juror based on the juror's race, he or she can make what's called a Batson challenge, named for *Batson v. Kentucky*, the case in which the U.S. Supreme Court made it illegal for prosecutors to reject potential jurors solely on that basis – which was permissible until 1986! When a lawyer makes a Batson challenge, the opposing counsel must defend his or her strike by proffering a non-racial reason.

Thus, if the second reviewer places an application in the "no" pile and notes that he went online and found that the applicant was convicted for driving under the influence, the first reviewer might reasonably trust that the rejection is fair. However, if the second reviewer's note says that the candidate "isn't conservatively groomed" or uses other particularly subjective language, the first reviewer should make a Batson challenge.

SECOND REVIEWER: What do you mean by "isn't conservatively groomed?"
FIRST REVIEWER: You know... not clean cut... wild looking hair.
SECOND REVIEWER: Describe "wild looking hair" for me.
FIRST REVIEWER: You know – it was halfway down his back and in those rope things.
SECOND REVIEWER: "Locs?"
FIRST REVIEWER: I guess.
SECOND REVIEWER: Okay, well, if that was the only concern, put him back in the "yes" pile.

From there, the first reviewer would use the technique in Chapter 2 for dealing with solipsism to explain that the organization's definition of conservative hairstyles must be broader simply than "hairstyles traditionally worn by white professionals." (Indeed, race-based hairstyle discrimination is a significant problem in workplaces and schools.)[32] For every subsequent round of the selection process through initial interviews to callbacks to the extension of final offers, disallow peremptory strikes and make Batson challenges.

(Note that when using this or other systems in this chapter, you may identify someone in your organization or community who has bias – for example, someone who consistently has pretexts for rejecting green candidates. When you notice disparate treatment, take action, whether that means calling someone's behavior to their attention and attempting to coach them to act equitably or expelling them for malicious prejudice.)

Sometimes, candidates – for employment, social organizations, etc. – are rejected for race-related reasons that decision-makers don't realize have any connection to color. For example, suppose Molly has a callback interview for a job at an investment bank that is held at an upscale steakhouse, so the employer can judge her etiquette, poise, and conversational skills to see if she has what it takes to court clients in a similar environment. Everything goes great, except when the waiter asks Molly how she'd like her steak prepared, she replies, "Well done, please." A few days after the interview, Molly learns that she's no longer in the running for the job.

What happened?

When applying for a job as an investment banker, attorney, consultant, etc. at an elite firm – or when being vetted for membership in an exclusive social organization – even a small faux pas can be a deal breaker. Ordering a steak well done is commonly seen as gauche among elite white Americans. For example, former president Donald Trump's preference for well done steak caused public outrage, and some used it to argue his unfitness for his role – acclaimed, white food writer Helen Rosner even argued, in perfect seriousness, that ordering a steak well done suggested character flaws that could be "catastrophic" for a president to possess.[33]

She wrote:

> Adults who won't eat pink-hearted steaks might lean on any number of reasons for their position, but almost always it comes down to an aversion to risk, which is at its core an unwillingness to trust the validity and goodwill of any experiences beyond the limited sphere of one's own.

Ironically, she – and decision-makers who make similar judgments – are guilty of the very solipsism they condemn. And that solipsism can have racial consequences. Because if Molly is African American, then she comes from a culture where ordering *pink* meat is commonly considered the faux pas.

To many African Americans, bloody meat is distasteful. Furthermore, even an African American who personally likes a rare or medium steak may consider it good manners to refrain from ordering it among people whose own preferences she does not know to avoid disgusting someone who may regard undercooked meat as repulsive. So, though Molly may have been rejected as unsavvy by white cultural standards, by African American ones, she exhibited savoir-faire. (And her etiquette would likely have been appreciated by potential African American clients.) Thus, in one sense, Molly wasn't rejected because she was African American. But in another sense, Molly was rejected because she was African American. To treat diverse people fairly, you must be culturally competent; thus, cultural competence training is a valuable investment.

Part of cultural competency is developing "cultural metacognition" or the ability to be aware of and think about one's cultural assumptions.[34] When we're culturally *incompetent*, we don't recognize our assumptions as such – rather, we mistake them for facts. Nor are we aware that what we presume to be facts are culturally inflected at all. Thus, a culturally incompetent person thinks, *This person is déclassé*. On the other hand, a culturally competent person may start to think, *This person is déclassé* as though the declaration were an objective fact before catching himself and realizing, *Wait! I'm making an* assumption *about this person because in my culture it's gauche to order a steak well done. However, the norms of her culture may be different.*

Cultural competency is not a white person *assuming* that a Black person who ordered a steak well done did so because she's Black or concluding that because the one Black person she knows also orders steaks well done, the behavior must be cultural. In this case, it's about a white person evaluating Molly's action from the starting point that the white person's interpretation of it is *informed by her own white culture.*

You may have heard, though, that cultural competency or anti-bias training doesn't work. But saying, "Anti-bias training doesn't work" is like saying, "There are no good, single men out there." It can *seem* that way sometimes, but, happily, it's not true.[35]

What *is* true is that not all cross-cultural training is created equal, so it's important to choose an evidence-based program. So, for what, according to science, should you look? Per a study in the American Psychological Association's *Psychological Bulletin*, "The positive effects of diversity training were greater when training was complemented by other diversity initiatives, targeted to both awareness and skills development, and conducted over a significant period of time."[36]

In other words, you can't just hire a diversity, equity, and inclusion specialist to put on a cross-cultural training and ignore other practices in this chapter – diversity training isn't like an inoculation that wards off prejudice in one "shot." It's more like exercise, meditation, or healthy eating – things that can improve our conditions *in conjunction* with other ameliorative efforts. And rehabilitating from the wound of racism is like rehabilitating from a physical injury – it takes more than one session. As for trainings being "targeted to both awareness and skills development," according to the study's authors,

> Awareness training focuses on getting participants to be more aware of their own and other cultural assumptions, values, and biases. Skill-building (behavioral) training educates participants on monitoring one's own

actions and appropriate responses to specific differences, such as identifying and overcoming interracial communication barriers (citations omitted).[37]

And remember, because the populations of organizations and communities are not static, diversity training needs to be part of newcomers' orientation.

But let's return to the subject of recruitment. Companies, are your internships paid or unpaid? Unpaid internships are only accessible to people who can support themselves and/or their families for an extended period without earning income. And that's a freedom many college students and even some teenagers (whose parents – or parent – may rely on their earnings to keep the household running or who are saving money for college) don't have. Furthermore, many internships require travel: In the United States, technology businesses are concentrated in Silicon Valley; investment banks, in New York City; and congressional work, exclusively in Washington, DC. The expenses of journeying between the town where one resides and the place of an internship and back at the program's beginning and end as well as the cost of living in cities that are often among the most expensive in the world can transform an internship from an investment in one's future into an unaffordable luxury, an imprudent gamble, or a crushing financial loss. When you offer an unpaid internship, unintentionally or not, your organization is basically saying, "The non-affluent need not apply."

So, how is this a racial issue? Because, in America, the median white family has twenty-two times more wealth than the median Latino family... and *forty-one* times more wealth than the median Black family.[38] In fact, the average white family has ten times the net worth of a non-white family.[39] So, anything that skews in favor of those with more financial resources also skews against people of color – and not insignificantly. Thus, unpaid internships are a form of affirmative action for whites. If your organization or your industry relies on people gaining a foot in the door through internships, then unpaid internships can blanche the complexion of an institution or even a whole field.

Pay interns.

Outside the company context, be mindful that if those who have more socio-economic privilege have more access to your community, then that means that those who are white have more access to it. If that bothers you, act. For example, a fraternity or sorority may consider if there's a way to lower dues. Or members might fundraise to offer "scholarships" to those who would otherwise be unable to afford joining. Or it might decide to place dues on a sliding scale. And social activities that require money such as eating off campus can be mixed with those that are free such as visiting a museum on a day with no entrance fees.

Furthermore, be careful not to mistake being underprivileged for a character flaw. I'll never forget what a Dartmouth cafeteria worker told me when I was writing her oral history, "Sometimes human resources will judge a job applicant as slovenly for wearing a torn coat to an interview... but that might be the only coat the applicant has."

Incidentally, the cafeteria worker who told me that was white and was discussing with me the experiences of underprivileged white people in New Hampshire... which raises an important point: A lot of the practices suggested in this chapter – and book – *directly benefit white people, too.*

But getting people of color into your organization or community is just the first step. Ensuring that they remain and attain is the next. Examine how your organization or community's culture may inadvertently disenfranchise people of certain races. For example, if, in an organization or industry, people find mentors, get career development advice, network, and forge key relationships on the golf course, then people who lack – or grew up without – the resources to play such as money for lessons or golf clubs or access to a golf course will be at a disadvantage. And again, those people will be disproportionately non-white. Similarly, if happy hour, wine tastings, breweries, or other alcohol-centric events are an important part of your firm or industry's culture, Muslims, who are forbidden to imbibe, and are likely to be non-white, will be disenfranchised.

But you can open the pathways to opportunity through simple tweaks: Switch between games of golf and a more accessible activity. Or instead of always gathering at the sports bar, alternate between spending time there and at a coffee shop. And regularly send out an anonymous survey about the accessibility of informal events. Remember though – even if you're not *in* authority, you still *have* the authority to make your company or community's culture more inclusive: Host accessible social gatherings in which you – and possibly like-minded peers – connect with those more junior than you and share the inside information about rising in the organization.

Pay attention to how people get mentors in your organization or community. Do senior people spontaneously choose when they want to cultivate someone more junior or are all new hires or community members (whether they be members of an arts company, postgraduate students, or priests, monks, nuns, etc.) assigned mentors? One problem with spontaneous mentorships is that, due to a phenomenon known as affinity bias, people commonly choose those who remind them of younger versions of themselves – which often involves inadvertent race and gender matching.[40] So, in an organization or community in which senior people are disproportionately or exclusively white, this can result in junior people who are disproportionately white being groomed for advancement. Other times, senior people feel drawn to nurture particular juniors based on qualities that can serve as unwitting proxies for race: the fact that both parties are alumni of the same disproportionately white prep school, members of the same disproportionately white fraternity or sorority, or that both play a white-dominated sport such as tennis or fencing. It is normal and by no means sinister for individuals to be drawn to those with whom they have things in common. The problem is that equally promising junior people of color who attended non-white schools or are members of non-white fraternities and sororities and have different hobbies may not attract the same attention and support. So, consider assigning each new hire or community member a mentor.

You may be concerned about taking this route, worried that mentorship relationships that don't arise "naturally" won't be dynamic and fruitful, but there are ways to make such relationships sincere and impactful. First, mentorships can still be based on mutual interests or similar qualities; have new hires and potential mentors fill out surveys listing what they're passionate about and match those who have things in common. A white woman who in the past has only mentored younger white women might get paired with a Native American man who shares her obsession with soccer. Or a white man who normally goes out of his way to support younger men who attended his disproportionately white fraternity might connect to an Asian woman because they're both passionate about cooking. My office assigns mentors based on personality and passion, which is how I, a multiracial woman of color with a master's degree in English and a doctorate focused on African American literature, ended up paired with a more senior white male attorney who has a doctorate in English and is a published poet.... We get along swimmingly.

And shared interests germane to the field or medium are – or rather *should be* – an obvious means of making connection: Due to their survey responses, junior and senior librarians might be paired based on their common interest in making the library more accessible to the disabled; curators, by their zeal for drawing younger generations into the museum; and members of a philanthropic organization, by a mutual enthusiasm for interfaith social justice initiatives.

You can also match people based on what they're looking to receive and what they have to give. For example, a new law associate who writes on a survey that "no one in my family or from the community I grew up in is an attorney, and I need someone to render the path to partnership less opaque" might be the perfect mentee for the partner who notes:

> I was the first person in my family to go to college. When I started my law career, things that everyone else seemed to know such as what type of suit is appropriate to wear to court or what "lockstep compensation" meant, I had no clue about. As a mentor, I'll tell my mentee the stuff I wish someone had told me.

But remember that a successful mentorship relationship is as much about logistics and communication styles as anything else. Consider matching people based on how – and how often – the parties would like to be in contact. Would the parties prefer a relationship in which they email each other occasionally as issues arise or one based on biweekly hour-long lunches or even one that includes the occasional karaoke night (like one partner/associate pair in my own office)?

You could also consider putting a formal, but non-obligatory, mentorship program in place beyond the work context. That's because in any realm in which there's a hierarchy to ascend or in which people need to "learn the ropes," some people will enter with more savvy than others. The woman whose parents and grandparents were members of an impactful and prestigious charitable society knows how to rise to its presidency – from which position she both has the clout to do good for the underprivileged and the cachet and networking opportunities to accrue further resources for the benefit of her *own* family and community. The self-made man who fought his way out of poverty may have uniquely insightful ideas on how to help vulnerable populations, but as a newbie in the organization, he might need someone to pull him aside and tell him that auctions raise more money than golf tournaments (or vice versa) or that summer is a poor time to hold a gala because invitees will be traveling. In such a context, willing experienced members of the charitable society could sign up to mentor new members interested in support and guidance.

However you pair mentors, and whatever their relationship looks like, make sure that all mentees are getting the same quality of support. Regularly give mentors and mentees a list of different types of engagement and ask them to check off those that they gave or received. For example, for a lawyer, items on the list might include "provided/received intensive feedback on a brief," "gave/received an opportunity for professional growth such as second chairing a deposition, managing discovery, or participating in a pitch to a client," or "explained/learned how to begin developing a book of business." By doing this, you have data you can use to make sure that certain demographics of mentees aren't being invested in less than others or that mentors don't treat mentees differently based on their race.

Also consider implementing a mentoring up program either on an institutional or individual level. In mentoring up relationships, a senior person learns from a junior person. Such programs spotlight the resources junior people have to share and put those talents on the radar of their superiors. They offer an added way for people on the lower rungs of the ladder to get noticed for their abilities – and for organizations to tap insights, skills, and gifts that might otherwise go overlooked. What this means is that such programs provide people from underrepresented backgrounds the opportunity to show what they have to offer, which, as I'll discuss later, is key to professional development. Thus, mentoring up benefits junior people, senior people, people from minority backgrounds, people from majority backgrounds, *and* the organization or community as a whole. Everybody wins.

Some things, however, shouldn't be left up to mentoring. In many organizations and communities, there are unwritten rules for success – for what it *really* takes to be named head of the academic department, get promoted to principal ballerina, rise from commis chef to chef de cuisine, or make partner at a law firm. To use the last example, if one of your parents was a lawyer, when you started work at a top civil litigation firm, he or she might have told you:

> Try to first chair a pro bono case – it will give you an opportunity to take a prominent role in court years earlier than you'll be allowed in a case for a paying client and give you a chance to show the partners what you can do.

On the other hand, if you're the first person in your family – or community – to be a lawyer, you might reasonably think that as long as you work exceedingly hard and do an exceptional job on the cases assigned to you, you're on the right track. A good mentor will whisper the advice about leading a pro bono case in your ear. But a fair firm makes the criteria for getting ahead explicit in the first place.

Why is this a racial justice issue? Because racially inequitable access to different arenas translates to racialized information gaps. So, in the legal context, a young attorney of color is less likely to have a relative in the practice who can offer career advice and may have senior colleagues who – again, given the complexion of the industry – are disproportionately likely to be white and, thus, may overlook her as a potential mentee for a white peer. But if everyone knows the rules of the game, then winning becomes more about who has the initiative and talent than who was handed a cheat sheet.

Track who gets the richest opportunities in your organization or community. To give an example from my own field – law – again, rising to partner depends on excelling at certain high-responsibility tasks. Yet, the way those tasks get assigned can be ad hoc and reflect affinity bias. Thus, it's all too easy for a white partner to unthinkingly fall into the pattern of asking the white associate who reminds the partner of a younger version of himself or herself to second chair the partner's deposition while only asking the non-white associate to do less flashy tasks such as research and document review. Of course, senior people can and should have the freedom to nurture more junior people they admire, but there also needs to be a system in place to check against unconscious bias – as well as intentional sidelining.

Create a list of what employees or community members need to execute to progress and keep track of the demographics of who gets the opportunity to perform. Review performance evaluations and make sure that similarly situated individuals from different demographics are given similar chances. Make senior people privy to the system that tracks who has earned the right to complete what tasks, who has been given the opportunity to take them on, and who is yet waiting, and keep track of how they assign duties. But even if your organization doesn't implement a top-down program for proffering opportunities equitably, you, and, possibly, any like-minded colleagues, can put an informal program in place for yourselves and your juniors – and if you do so, talk up the benefits to inspire wider adoption of the practice!

What else should you be tracking? The speed at which people of different races rise under different superiors and what it takes for them to do so... per the aforementioned proverb, do people of color have to work twice as hard to get half as far? The length of time that they stay in your organization or community. The reasons that they leave – so that, if necessary, you can remedy them. How often people of different races are disciplined, what they're disciplined for, and by whom. To the foregoing, Hirsh and Tomaskovic-Devey also suggest tracking to make sure there are not racial disparities in pay and recording "internal and external complaints of discrimination, bias, and harassment as well as managers' responses."[41]

You may have seen the title of Chief Diversity Officer and wondered what such a person does. Well, in part... *this*. But, you don't need a Chief Diversity Officer to do this work. Your organization could delegate these duties as it would any other managerial tasks.

You may also be reading this thinking – I see how *some* organizations or communities or individuals could benefit from a tool like this, but *my* company or *I* don't need it. And you could be right. But it's worth it to check. Have you ever tried tracking everything you eat in a week? You might wholeheartedly understand the value of healthy eating, want to eat healthy, like to eat healthy, and *think* you eat healthy... but once you write down everything that passes your lips, you realize, *Gee, I eat a ton of French fries. Do I seriously snack on cookies that much? I was under the impression that I ate a lot of vegetables.* Or maybe you find that you're doing a lot of things right, but there are some things you could do better that would have a significant impact on your health – that if you cut down on salt and drank more water, it would really make a positive difference.

Our behavior toward race is similar – we can understand the value of being antiracist, want to be antiracist, and *think* we're being antiracist, but once we track what we actually *do*, we can see whether we're *actually* furthering the cause of racial justice. And we can see how we can improve. To take the illustration a step further, a health-conscious woman takes steps such as eating nutritious food and exercising to lower her risk of breast cancer... but she also gets mammograms to check whether, despite her efforts, she has it. Antiracists take steps to be equitable and inclusive, but they don't blindly assume that those efforts take care of the problem. They check.

There are some things that you can't track but of which you *can* be mindful. Reflect upon on what rising in your organization is contingent. For example, in fields such as law and finance, promotion can depend, in significant part, on one's ability to develop business, bring in clients, or recruit investors – lawyers at elite firms may be expected to bring in legal clients who are suing or being sued for a minimum of two million dollars. And they're commonly advised to find such people through their social circles – to reach out to the people they went to school with, their relatives, etc. Very few white people went to school with or come from families that have multimillion-dollar legal problems, yet, in America, they are exponentially more likely to originate from such a background than non-whites. In countries that have racial wealth gaps and de facto segregation, it is racial injustice to condition promotion essentially on an employee's proximity to wealth. Furthermore, doing so *perpetuates* the racial wealth gap – those with racial-economic privilege rise to the top of their fields and accrue resources that remain concentrated away from non-white communities for yet another generation.

Thus, if you have a company in which employees need to bring in wealthy businesses or individuals as clients or investors to ascend, you need to recognize that for some people – people who are disproportionately non-white – advice such as "mention what you do when you're at cocktail parties" is worthless. Train *all* your people on ways to generate business or bring in clients or investors that aren't contingent upon coming from racial and/or economic privilege – regularly bring in speakers who specialize in the subject, recommend books, etc. And when it comes time to make decisions about promotion, be mindful that the person who has to become a thought leader in his or her field to generate business or acquire clients and investors is always going to be at a disadvantage to the person who can just call up his dad's golf buddies. Judge people by their efforts and their effectiveness – don't penalize them for having the poor judgment to be born into races whose labor, wealth, and resources were stolen by slavery, colonial land theft, and unjust laws such as the exclusion of domestics and agricultural laborers from the Social Security Act of 1935 (which denied Social Security pensions and benefits to three-fourths of Black workers).[42]

Even here, though, data has a role to play. Since you are tracking the numbers of people of each race at the various levels of your organization as well as how quickly it takes them to rise, their skill levels, and why they were promoted (*right?*), you can see if attorneys of color are stalling at the rank of senior associate, counsel, or of counsel, while whites are more likely to proceed to partner and investigate the cause and innovate a remedy for any disparity.

But being mindful of the racial wealth gap goes beyond the workplace. For example, museums, arts institutions, charitable organizations, private schools, universities, and other such entities are the pillars of civic life, and they're run by boards. But many boards have a policy of "give, get, or get off" meaning that members must either personally donate (give) or successfully fundraise (get donations) to the organization in order not to be forced to get off the board. However, because of our nemesis, the racial wealth gap, white Americans are far more likely to have the assets to give and the connections to get… which means non-whites are far less likely to get a seat at the table, less likely to be in the position to have a say in how their communities are educated and enriched. It means that the way the museum portrays the history we all learn or the way the university engages in the medical research we all depend upon is disproportionately determined by one race. It means that the people who decide whether the faculty hiring or admissions policies at the university are racially just or – who fail to think to address the issue altogether – are disproportionately white. But power shouldn't be racially concentrated.

And right now it is. In 2017, eighty-four percent of board members in America were white,[43] even though whites are just seventy-six percent of the population. Thus, boards should amend their policies to expand what it means to give. By valuing people who can contribute governance skills and not just financial resources,[44] you can make your board – and the organization it leads – more racially just. In any realm in which financial privilege serves to exclude, be mindful of the racial consequences of that exclusion and look for ways to be inclusive.

Even if your organization or community doesn't exclude people of other races, make sure it doesn't inadvertently penalize antiracist work. Again, I'll provide an example from the law firm context. If a law firm encourages its employees to engage in diversity, equity, and inclusion efforts – to serve on the firm's diversity council, to recruit lawyers from underrepresented backgrounds, to publish articles on civil rights in legal journals – but compensates and promotes lawyers based not on those things but on the hours they bill and the business they bring in, then the firm is actually *penalizing* antiracist work. Everyone has the same twenty-four hours in his or her day, and every hour spent donating one's time to give a lecture on responding to racial profiling at the meeting of the local ethnic organization is an hour one can't spend on billing a client – and, thus, an hour one has taken away from contributing to the year-end bonus he or she relies on to save up for a child's college education or a house and an hour head start given to the colleague one is competing against for partner. And those hours add up. Meanwhile, the firm is making hip social media posts about its commitment to justice, getting acclaimed for the diversity of its attorneys (and wooing clients who increasingly demand that diverse advocates represent them before diverse juries), and using those law review articles to promote itself in the public sphere. *Its* status and profits are going up all the while the status and compensation of the antiracist lawyer responsible for the benefits to the firm are going down. Worse, it's often non-whites who shoulder the responsibility for doing antiracist work, so it's they who bear the toll of that work even as people of all races share the benefit.

At my firm, a certain amount of hours spent working on behalf of the diversity for the firm – for example, of the hours I serve on the Firm Diversity Council – is remunerated the same as billable hours spent serving a client. Furthermore, whether one is on the Council or not, work to make the firm more diverse, equitable, and inclusive is considered all lawyers' responsibility... and is a criteria for promotion.

This practice should be more widespread. From individuals, like the history professor who was one of the few Native American faculty members during my time at Yale, who, in addition to the research, teaching, and History Department responsibilities he shared with his colleagues, was also the de facto (and unpaid) head of Native American recruitment and a quasi-dean of diversity for the entire University – including me and my fellow Native American *law students* – to the Black, Hispanic, and Asian American custodians and cafeteria workers at my prep school, who, in addition to taking excellent care of the campus and making wonderful meals, went out of their way to nurture me, my sister, and the handful of students of color, people of character – who are often people of color – build the value of our communities and companies through their efforts.

So, they deserve to reap dividends.

Until this point in the chapter, we've dealt with how organizations and communities can go about changing *who* they are. Now, we'll discuss transforming *how* they are.

First, from the moment you engage a real estate agent to find the plot for your institution – or a web developer to create your site, recognize that purchasing power is never a neutral force. The Association for Enterprise Opportunity reports that "Black business owners have a median net worth 12 times higher than a black person who doesn't own a business...." Although correlation is not causation, the statistic suggests that entrepreneurship enriches people of African descent. What's more, the government is the number one employer of Blacks... Black businesses are the second.[45] So when you buy Black – or brown... you shrink that wealth gap down....

Laysha Ward, executive vice president and chief external engagement officer at Target, counsels leaders to recognize that:

> Purchasing power is one important way to address issues of wealth creation and jobs. Assess your supply chain from multiple angles and design a supplier diversity program that reflects your brand, your racial equity strategy, and the communities you serve. Ensure the right mix of BIPOC [Black, Indigenous, People of Color] and local vendors — not just for raw materials or products but also for services like legal, marketing, and IT.[46]

So, draft a racial justice budget. For example, you could make your spending reflect population parity. Thus, since Latinos are eighteen percent of the U.S. population, a nationwide business might plan to spend eighteen percent of its outflow with Latino vendors, and so on and so forth for other racial groups. But don't *just* plan – balance the books. Remember, to manage diversity effectively, you must hold people to account for metrics, so it's not enough to *intend* to support vendors of color. Someone should be held just as responsible for ensuring that your organization didn't go underbudget in terms of racially just spending as he or she is for ensuring it didn't go overbudget in paying for goods and services.

And when engaging *white* vendors, choose those who support diversity. How can you tell whether they do? Definitely not by checking for a diversity statement on the company's website or social media. Look for hard data. For example, in the United States, many businesses are required by law to fill out EEO-1 reports that disclose race and gender demographic data for different job categories. Such reports are "the 'gold standard' for diversity disclosure."[47] Hirsh and Tomaskovic-Devey advise those companies not legally bound to submit EEO-1s to draft and make public similar reports.[48] *Your* company, of course, should also engage in such reporting.

I'm particularly inspired by the example set by corporate litigation clients. In the past few years, major companies have realized that American juries, which, reflecting demographic changes, are increasingly made up of racial minorities, pay attention to the races of corporations' lawyers. They notice the army of attorneys sitting at the plaintiff's of defense's table… and they notice when not one of them is non-white. At the same time, people of color have fought like military generals to achieve the role of general counsel (head in-house lawyers) at top businesses. They're the ones who decide which outside counsel to hire when the businesses for which they work must handle a lawsuit or a merger – and they aren't impressed when elite firms send all-white pitch teams that the general counsels *know* are not representative of the talent pool. Nor are they fooled when a token attorney of color is brought to a pitch only to sit silently in the boardroom like a prop while the work of marketing the firm's services is entrusted only to his or her white colleagues. Principled white general counsels aren't amused either.

So increasingly, some of the most powerful corporations in America demand to see that significant numbers of people of color (and women) are *substantively* involved in their litigation from the pitch meeting on, even going so far as to review billable hour invoices to make sure that the diverse attorneys on their cases aren't relegated to grunt work. Their assiduousness is an example for all of us.

And that includes individuals – keep a personal or household racial budget. Before you make a purchase, do an online search for wholesalers and retailers of color. Sometimes antiracists fill their children's libraries with picture books by non-white authors and illustrators, but forget they can also buy mundane things, like detergent, from the same populations.

Put your money in a Black bank. As Maggie Anderson, author of *Our Black Year: One Family's Quest to Buy Black in America's Racially Divided Economy* quips, such institutions are FDIC-insured just like their white counterparts![49] Hire an Asian lawyer to draft your will. Get your kids a Hispanic pediatrician. I remember how, on the first day of Spanish class in kindergarten, students excitedly told our teacher, "My maid speaks Spanish!" If their parents had made a point of integrating people of color from a variety of vocations into their lives, they might have instead enthused that their *doctors* spoke Spanish.

Where you site your organization also matters. Food deserts – neighborhoods that lack access to affordable, healthy nourishment – are more common in the communities of racial minorities.[50] So if you put your grocery store in such a community, you can do well and do good. On the other hand, be mindful of things such as environmental racism, defined by civil rights leader Benjamin Chavis:

> as racial discrimination in environmental policy-making and enforcement of regulations and laws, the deliberate targeting of communities of color for toxic waste facilities, the official sanctioning of the presence of life threatening [sic] poisons and pollutants for communities of color, and the history of excluding people of color from leadership of the environmental movement.[51]

Don't site your business in a way that concentrates pollution in a non-white community. Basically, in locating your organization, seek to remedy – or at least not exacerbate – the fact that communities of color often have less than their share of benefits – such as healthy food and clean air and geographically accessible jobs[52] – and more than their share of afflictions such as pollution.

We've talked about the vendors your organization might use and where it might be located, but what about what your organization actually *does*? Say your organization is a bank. As I noted at the beginning of this chapter, controlling for socio-economics, non-whites are less likely to be given mortgage loans than whites. So, an antiracist bank should track the race of applicants, their socio-economic disposition, which loan officers served them and the officers' races, whether the loan was approved or denied, the loans' interest rates, and any other relevant factors. That way any racial disparities – and racial discrimination – can be identified and remedied.

Then the bank would proceed to examine its investing practices. For example, the U.S. House Committee on Financial Services found:

> Despite evidence that women and minority-owned firms perform as well as (and sometimes outperform) their industry counterparts… women and minority-owned firms account for approximately 8.6 percent of the asset management industry, [but] recent reports show that they only manage 1.1 percent of all assets under management or $785 billion out of $71.4 trillion, and are underrepresented as managers in every asset class.[53]

Thus, the bank should set *and adhere to* SMART diversity investment targets. And so forth. Every element of the bank's – or any organization's – practice vulnerable to racial disparity should involve *metrics, accountability,* and, where appropriate, *targets*. Think of it this way: Go to the MAT for racial justice.

Going to the MAT might have prevented the Metropolitan Opera, the largest opera house in the United States, from reaching the fall of 2020 without producing a single opera by a Black composer over the course of its one hundred thirty-seven years.[54]

Going to the MAT might have prevented a literary realm in which ninety-five percent of English language fiction books in print from major publishers are white.[55]

Of course, this dystopian reality is not disjunctive from the fact that the heads of all the major publishing houses are white as well as eighty-five percent of editors – who not only revise but also choose which books get published.[56] And perhaps it would not be going too far to suggest that the Met's production history is linked to the fact that only three of the forty-five managing directors, one of the ten music staff, and two of the ninety orchestra members are Black.[57]

That's why unweaving systemic racism is about transforming who you are and how you are.

So, remember: Making a *statement* affirming racial justice doesn't create profound transformation.

Implementing *systems* to achieve racial equity *does*.

Notes

1 "MCI Tracks Corporate America's Early Response to BLM," American Marketing Association, last modified September 8, 2020, https://www.ama.org/marketing-news/mci-tracks-corporate-americas-early-response-to-blm/.
2 Emmanuel Martinez and Aaron Glantz, *How Reveal Identified Lending Disparities in Federal Mortgage Data* (Emeryville, CA: Reveal from the Center for Investigative Reporting, 2018), https://s3-us-west-2.amazonaws.com/revealnews.org/uploads/lending_disparities_whitepaper_180214.pdf.
3 "Diversity and Inclusion: Holding America's Large Banks Accountable," U.S. House Committee on Financial Services, last modified February 2020, https://financialservices.house.gov/issues/diversity-and-inclusion-holding-americas-large-banks-accountable.htm.
4 Karsten Strauss, "More Evidence That Company Diversity Leads to Better Profits," *Forbes*, January 25, 2018, https://www.forbes.com/sites/karstenstrauss/2018/01/25/more-evidence-that-company-diversity-leads-to-better-profits/?sh=3a6a3e891bc7.
5 Alia Wong, "Why Are There So Few Black Children in Gifted Programs?" *The Atlantic*, January 19, 2016, https://www.theatlantic.com/education/archive/2016/01/why-are-there-so-few-black-children-in-gifted-and-talented-programs/424707/.
6 Stuart R. Levine, "Diversity Confirmed to Boost Innovation and Financial Results," *Forbes*, January 15, 2020, https://www.forbes.com/sites/forbesinsights/2020/01/15/diversity-confirmed-to-boost-innovation-and-financial-results/?sh=34be146cc4a6.
7 Elizabeth Hirsh and Donald Tomaskovic-Devey, "Metrics, Accountability, and Transparency: A Simple Recipe to Increase Diversity and Reduce Bias," in *What Works: Evidence-Based Ideas to Increase Diversity, Equity, and Inclusion in the Workplace* (Amherst, MA: Center for Employment Equity, 2020), https://www.umass.edu/employmentequity/sites/default/files/What_Works.pdf.
8 See Mary Szto, "Real Estate Agents as Agents of Social Change: Redlining, Reverse Redlining, and Greenlining," *Seattle Journal for Social Justice* 12, no. 1 (2013): 1–59, https://digitalcommons.law.seattleu.edu/sjsj/vol12/iss1/2.

9 "Quick Facts: United States," United States Census Bureau, October 22, 2020, https://www.census.gov/quickfacts/fact/table/US/PST045219.
10 Deborah L. Rhode, "Law Is the Least Diverse Profession in the Nation. And Lawyers Aren't Doing Enough to Change That," *The Washington Post*, May 27, 2015, https://www.washingtonpost.com/posteverything/wp/2015/05/27/law-is-the-least-diverse-profession-in-the-nation-and-lawyers-arent-doing-enough-to-change-that/.
11 "Cultivating Exceptional Lawyers Who Also Happen to Be Diverse," Pipeline to Practice Foundation, last modified Spring 2020, https://pipelinetopractice.org/wp-content/uploads/2020/06/Spring-2020-P2P-Impact-Statement-1.pdf.
12 "Project Plié," American Ballet Theater, January 6, 2021, https://support.abt.org/projectplie.
13 Hye Jin Rho, Hayley Brown, and Shawn Fremstad, *A Basic Demographic Profile of Workers in Frontline Industries* (Washington, DC: Center for Economic and Policy Research, 2020), https://cepr.net/wp-content/uploads/2020/04/2020-04-Frontline-Workers.pdf.
14 "Section 15 Race and Color Discrimination," U.S. Equal Employment Opportunity Commissioner, October 20, 2020, https://www.eeoc.gov/laws/guidance/section-15-race-and-color-discrimination#N_84_.
15 Kristen Chick, "Pulpit Swap: What Happens When Churches Switch Preachers?" *The Christian Science Monitor*, April 28, 2010, https://www.csmonitor.com/USA/2010/0428/Pulpit-swap-What-happens-when-churches-switch-preachers.
16 Misty Copeland, *Life in Motion: An Unlikely Ballerina* (New York: Touchstone, 2014), 38, 43.
17 "Children's Internet Access at Home," The Condition of Education, National Center for Education Statistics, last modified May 2020, https://nces.ed.gov/programs/coe/indicator_cch.asp.
18 Jeremy Ashkenas, Haeyoun Park, and Adam Pearce, "Even with Affirmative Action, Blacks and Hispanics Are More Underrepresented at Top Colleges Than 35 Years Ago," *New York Times*, August 24, 2017, https://www.nytimes.com/interactive/2017/08/24/us/affirmative-action.html?hp&action=click&pgtype=Homepage&clickSource=story-heading&module=photo-spot-region&region=top-news&WT.nav=top-news&_r=0.
19 Stephen B. Oates, *Let the Trumpet Sound: A Life of Martin Luther King, Jr.* (New York: HarperPerennial, 1994), 426.
20 Marin Wolf and Kim Bhasin, "Wells Fargo, Delta Join a Nascent Push into Racial Hiring Quotas," *Bloomberg*, September 1, 2020, https://www.bloomberg.com/news/articles/2020-09-01/can-quotas-fix-diversity-these-major-companies-hope-so.
21 Devah Pager, "The Mark of a Criminal Record," *AJS* 108, no. 5 (March 2003): 958, https://scholar.harvard.edu/files/pager/files/pager_ajs.pdf. Another study found that Asian and Black candidates who "whiten" their resumes – for example by using a Western name instead of an Asian one or by omitting references to Black professional associations, were far more likely to get callbacks than those who did not; Asians were nearly twice as likely, and Blacks were two and a half times more likely. Sonia K. Kang, Katherine A. DeCelles, András Tilcsik, and Sora Jun, "Whitened Résumés: Race and Self-Presentation in the Labor Market," *Administrative Science Quarterly* 63, no. 3 (September 2016): 470, https://doi.org/10.1177/0001839216639577.
22 Sean Thomas-Breitfeld and Frances Kunreuther, *Race to Lead: Confronting the Nonprofit Racial Leadership Gap* (New York: Building Movement Project, 2017), https://racetolead.org/wp-content/uploads/2017/12/RacetoLeadNonprofitRacialLeadershipGap-3.pdf.

23 Strauss, "Evidence."
24 Christine Simmons, "170 GCs Pen Open Letter to Law Firms: Improve on Diversity or Lose Our Business," *The American Lawyer*, January 27, 2019, https://www.law.com/americanlawyer/2019/01/27/170-gcs-pen-open-letter-to-law-firms-improve-on-diversity-or-lose-our-business/; Amy McMillan-Capehart, Joshua R. Aaron, and Brandon N. Cline, "Investor Reactions to Diversity Reputation Signals," *Corporate Reputation Review* 13, no. 13 (2010): 184, 193, https://www.researchgate.net/profile/Amy-Mcmillan-2/publication/47464282_Investor_Reactions_to_Diversity_Reputation_Signals/links/54db80aa0cf261ce15d03499/Investor-Reactions-to-Diversity-Reputation-Signals.pdf; Vivian Hunt, Dennis Layton, and Sara Prince, *Diversity Matters* (McKinsey & Company, 2015), https://www.insurance.ca.gov/diversity/41-ISDGBD/GBDExternal/upload/McKinseyDivmatters-201501.pdf; David Rock and Heidi Grant, "Why Diverse Teams are Smarter," *Harvard Business Review*, November 4, 2016, https://hbr.org/2016/11/why-diverse-teams-are-smarter.
25 Joan C. Williams and James D. White, "Update Your DE&I Playbook," *Harvard Business Review*, July 15, 2020, https://hbr.org/2020/07/update-your-dei-playbook.
26 Wolf and Bhasin, "Quotas."
27 William Lauder and Fabrizio Freda, "November 2020 Progress Update: ELC's Commitment to Racial Equity," *Estée Lauder Companies*, November 16, 2020, https://www.elcompanies.com/en/news-and-media/newsroom/company-features/2020/elc-commits-to-racial-equity-nov.
28 Ibid.
29 The Times Editorial Board, "Prop 16: California Votes against Affirmative Action – again," *Los Angeles Times*, November 5, 2020, https://www.latimes.com/opinion/story/2020-11-05/proposition-16-fails-affirmative-action.
30 Helene Cooper, "Addressing Diversity, Army Will Remove Photos of Officer Candidates in Promotion Reviews," *New York Times*, June 25, 2020, https://www.nytimes.com/2020/06/25/us/politics/army-pentagon-race-promotions.html.
31 Gilad Edelman, "Why Is It So Easy for Prosecutors to Strike Black Jurors?" *The New Yorker*, June 5, 2015, https://www.newyorker.com/news/news-desk/why-is-it-so-easy-for-prosecutors-to-strike-black-jurors.
32 "Creating a Respectful and Open World for Natural Hair," The Crown Act, January 6, 2021, https://www.thecrownact.com/.
33 Helen Rosner, "Actually, How Donald Trump Eats His Steak Matters," *Eater*, February 28, 2017, https://www.eater.com/2017/2/28/14753248/trump-steak-well-done-ketchup-personality.
34 Michael W. Morris, "Metacognition: The Skill Every Global Leader Needs," *Harvard Business Review*, October 17, 2012, https://hbr.org/2012/10/collaborating-across-cultures.
35 Katerina Bezrukova, Chester S. Spell, Jamie L. Perry, and Karen A. Jehn, "A Meta-Analytical Integration of over 40 Years of Research on Diversity Training Evaluation," *Psychological Bulletin* 142, no. 11 (2016): 1227, http://dx.doi.org/10.1037/bul0000067.
36 Ibid.
37 Ibid., 1231.
38 Chuck Collins, Dedrick Asante-Muhammed, Josh Hoxie, and Sabrina Terry, *Dreams Deferred: How Enriching the 1% Widens the Racial Wealth Divide* (Washington, DC: Institute for Policy Studies, 2019), https://inequality.org/wp-content/uploads/2019/01/IPS_RWD-Report_FINAL-1.15.19.pdf.

39 Catholic Charities USA, *Poverty and Racism: Overlapping Threats to the Common Good* (Alexandria, VA: Catholic Charities USA, 2020), https://www.catholiccharitiesusa.org/wp-content/uploads/2020/08/Poverty-and-Racism-2020_FINAL.pdf.
40 Monica Thakar, "Unconscious Bias and Three Ways to Overcome It," *Forbes*, November 19, 2018, https://www.forbes.com/sites/forbescoachescouncil/2018/11/19/unconscious-bias-and-three-ways-to-overcome-it/?sh=3207fe342677.
41 Hirsh and Tomaskovic-Devey, "Metrics, Accountability, and Transparency."
42 Catholic Charities USA, *Poverty and Racism*.
43 BoardSource, *Taking on Board Diversity: Five Questions to Get You Started* (Washington, DC: BoardSource.org, 2017), https://boardsource.org/wp-content/uploads/2017/09/5-Questions-for-board-diversity-2.pdf?utm_referrer=https%3A%2F%2Fboardsource.org%2Ftaking-action-board-diversity-five-questions-get-started%2F.
44 William P. Ryan, "Myth: Good Board Members 'Give, Get, or Get Off'," *Nonprofit Quarterly*, July 23, 2005, https://nonprofitquarterly.org/myth-good-board-members-give-get-or-get-off/.
45 Anthonia Akitunde, "Buying Black, Rebooted," *New York Times*, December 26, 2019, https://www.nytimes.com/2019/12/25/style/buying-black-rebooted.html.
46 Laysha Ward, "What an Anti-Racist Business Strategy Looks Like," *Harvard Business Review*, November 30, 2020, https://hbr.org/2020/11/what-an-anti-racist-business-strategy-looks-like.
47 Jena McGregor, "Urged to Back up Pledges for Racial Justice, 34 Major Firms Commit to Disclose Government Workforce Data," *The Washington Post*, September 29, 2020, https://www.washingtonpost.com/business/2020/09/29/corporate-diversity-data-pledge/.
48 Hirsh and Tomaskovic-Devey, "Metrics, Accountability, and Transparency."
49 Maggie Anderson and Ted Gregory, *Our Black Year: One Family's Quest to Buy Black in America's Racially Divided Economy* (New York: PublicAffairs, 2012), 229.
50 See Kelly M. Bower, Roland J. Thorpe, Charles Rohde, and Darrell J. Gaskin, "The Intersection of Neighborhood Racial Segregation, Poverty, and Urbanicity and Its Impact on Food Store Availability in the United States," *Preventive Medicine*, 58 (January 2014): 33–39, https://doi.org/10.1016/j.ypmed.2013.10.010.
51 Ryan Holifield, "Defining Environmental Justice and Environmental Racism," *Urban Geography* 22, no. 1 (2001): 83, https://doi.org/10.2747/0272-3638.22.1.78.
52 Michael A. Stoll and Kenya Covington, "Explaining Racial/Ethnic Gaps in Spatial Mismatch in the US: The Primacy of Racial Segregation," *Urban Studies* 49, no. 11 (November 2012): 2501–2521. https://doi.org/10.1177/0042098011427180.
53 U.S. House Committee on Financial Services, "Banks."
54 Joshua Barone, "Opera Can No Longer Ignore Its Race Problem," *New York Times*, September 23, 2020, https://www.nytimes.com/2020/07/16/arts/music/opera-race-representation.html?action=click&module=RelatedLinks&pgtype=Article.
55 Richard Jean So and Gus Wezerek, "Just How White Is the Book Industry?" *New York Times*, December 11, 2020, https://www.nytimes.com/interactive/2020/12/11/opinion/culture/diversity-publishing-industry.html.
56 Ibid.
57 Barone, "Opera."

Chapter 4

Reckoning with the past

As a Fellow at Auschwitz for the Study of Professional Ethics, I visited the eponymous Holocaust death camp. I didn't think to myself what a delightful place it would be to hold a wedding.

I didn't imagine how cool it would be if I could take a "haunted" tour of the camp and hear the prisoners' anguish spun into entertainingly gruesome ghost stories.

I didn't fantasize about wearing period clothing and living in the romantic days of the Third Reich.

I cried.

Yet when non-Blacks visit the plantations where my ascendants were enslaved – the concentration camps where they did not simply die in slavery but *of* slavery, within a system, though not of extermination, of disposability,[1] those visitors commonly react in those ways that would have been anathema to me, engaging in Holocaust denial and even in Holocaust celebration.

No one at Auschwitz was confused about what was and wasn't appropriate. The norms that governed behavior there were both implicit and intuitive. Yet somehow, the standards surrounding statues, symbols, or sites related to atrocities suffered by people of color are not.

Thus, our organizations and communities echo with anxious inquiries as to what we should do about Columbus Day or Confederate flags.

To those queries, I have a radical answer:

We should do what we do when victims were or are white.

This chapter takes seriously the idea that all men and women are created equal, and it invites you to lead your organization or community through issues of celebration, reparation, and reckoning governed by just one principle: that people who are not white are of identical moral worth to those who are.

So, should your workplace allow Confederate flags?

Not if it wouldn't permit swastikas.

But how do you get your organization or community to agree with that and transform itself accordingly? Greg Satell researched people who practice changemaking – in organizations, through social movements, and even through political revolution. Here's what he found successful efforts have in

DOI: 10.4324/9781003144298-5

common: First, changemakers begin by mobilizing a small group of people who share their values.[2] As described in Chapter 3, at my law firm, in the wake of George Floyd's killing, lawyers and staff members passionate about antiracism had conversations amongst ourselves about how the firm could make its preexisting commitment to racial justice even more robust. Then, we reached out to leadership, who responded by implementing a range of initiatives to make both the firm and society more diverse, equitable, and inclusive.

Second, changemakers turn a grievance into a vision initially realized through a "keystone change" that is concrete, "involves multiple stakeholders, and paves the way for bigger changes down the road."[3] The Episcopal Diocese of New York's problem was that it had been complicit with slavery, segregation, and discrimination. Its vision, which cited to Bernice Powell Jackson, Executive Minister for Justice Ministry of the United Church of Christ's definition of "reparations," was to engage in a process "to remember, repair, restore, reconcile and make amends…." Its keystone change was to appoint a Reparations Committee (a small group of the sort described in Step one) to research the Diocese's history and the benefits it derived from slavery in order to "discern a process toward restorative justice."[4] That committee has included multiple stakeholders such as Black civil rights activist Nell Gibson and white reverend Chuck Kramer.[5] And, as noted, the very commission of the Committee was to pave the way for further change.

Third, changemakers "woo" others to their cause, creating "an ecosystem of stakeholders." This is exactly what the antiracists at my firm did.[6] Leaders fired up the members of the organization to get active in diversity, equity, and inclusion efforts by sharing inspiring stories of the firm's racial justice legacy and making us feel not just like owners or employees but protagonists in a quest for a better tomorrow. People throughout the organization were eager to participate in the firm's growth from the affinity groups for Asian American and Pacific Islanders, Hispanics, Blacks, LGBT lawyers and allies, and women to members of the newly created Firm Diversity Council to partners who saw supporting diversity, equity, and inclusion as part and parcel of their leadership duties to staff who felt the same commitment.

Fourth, rather than resting on their laurels, changemakers recognize the need for continued evolution and improvement.[7] This is the attitude at my firm. For example, we're proud of our Mansfield 3.0 Certification – of being a law firm that has committed to thirty percent of the candidates for leadership roles and major opportunities being women, people with disabilities, LGBTQ+, or attorneys of color. (When firms commit simply to *consider* attorneys from these demographics for competitive roles and responsibilities, those attorneys earn those roles and responsibilities at increased rates.)[8] But on the Firm Diversity Council, we're exploring further ways to recruit and develop lawyers from marginalized backgrounds, and ensure their talents and performance are assessed fairly. Our ethos isn't to *settle* on a solution but to *strive*, to cultivate a corporate culture in which we're always looking for – or in the process of creating – the next best thing. As Satell notes, successful changemakers "focus not only on immediate goals but also the process of change itself… to keep moving forward."[9]

All that said, if you want to make change but don't have support, there are ways to do so which I'll discuss in the next chapter.

Now let's discuss the changes you may want to make. In the spirit of my proffered principle that people who are not white are of identical moral worth to those who *are* white, when you're trying to help your organization or community decide whether it's appropriate to celebrate gross human rights violations or those who committed them, one tactic you can use is to appeal to the norm your institution probably *already has* and ask for it to be applied uniformly – regardless of the race of the victims. Point out that to treat crimes against humanity as less abhorrent when perpetrated upon people of color than upon whites is to hold that people of color are less human than whites and that our discrepancies in handling the past are responsible for the disparities we face in the present.

However, some people wonder about the consequences of knocking malefactors off their metaphorical and literal pedestals. For example, as former president Trump warned in the wake of the movement to remove monuments to Confederates, "Now they are even trying to destroy statues of Christopher Columbus. What's next?"[10] Mind you, one would be hard pressed to think of someone *less* worthy of being honored than a man whose résumé of barbarities includes the annihilation of Haiti's indigenous people *and* commencing the transatlantic slave trade.[11] Nevertheless, the answer to the question of "What's next?" is, "What's next is a society in which indigenous peoples, Blacks, and others are spared the indignity of the glorification of those who exterminated or enslaved them – *just as white people are*."

Thus, when confronted with a slippery slope "what's next" argument, point out the double standard. Flag the discrepancy that allows one to take the absence of honors to those who committed gross abuses of whites as a given yet rejects the pursuit of a similar absence of honors to those who committed gross abuses of non-whites as fanatical excess.

You can help your organization think through the issue of celebrating white supremacy by facilitating a conversation, *politely* asking questions that help your community first, articulate its values, and then, analyze whether its policies and practices reflect them. For example, suppose your company is grappling with the issue of whether Confederate flags should be flown by the institution, allowed on the premises, used on products, or permitted in other contexts. After having prepared for the conversation by thoroughly researching the history of the Confederate flag as well as the most common apologia for displaying it, you might begin with a remark such as:

> I know we have a few veterans working here. I know we also have a couple of people whose children are currently serving in the military.

> I spend my Saturdays volunteering, tutoring kids, because that's my way of investing in the future of this country, and I understand a lot of you are active in your churches, do community service, or help your neighbors – that you give of yourselves in the quiet ways that make our nation strong. Would I be correct in calling "patriotism" a value we share as an organization?

After laying this foundation, a follow-up question would be "Does glorifying people who seceded from our country affirm or violate that value?"

Someone may assert that Confederates *were* American patriots. Indeed, historian John Coski has described how the Confederate flag has been treated as a "second American flag" by those who feel a "dual loyalty" to the United States and the nation that rebelled against it[12] – almost as though those people consider themselves to hold dual citizenship. In response to such an argument, follow-up questions could be: How can patriotism, which means devotion to one's country, encompass treason against one's country? If *treason* isn't unpatriotic, what is? Use the technique of unveiling dissonance, as described in Chapter 2, to highlight the tension between the value being championed and the behavior being defended.

Ask what values the practice being challenged affirmed and whether those values are in concert with the community's. In this case, one would query which tenets Confederates championed. If you are given an inaccurate answer such as "states' rights,"[13] cite to history, for example, the Cornerstone Speech, an address given by Confederate Vice President Alexander H. Stephens, in which he declared:

> The [United States] constitution [sic], it is true, secured every essential guarantee to the institution while it should last, and hence no argument can be justly urged against the constitutional guarantees thus secured, because of the common sentiment of the day. Those ideas, however, were fundamentally wrong. They rested upon the assumption of the equality of races. This was an error. It was a sandy foundation, and the government built upon it fell when the "storm came and the wind blew."
>
> Our new government is founded upon exactly the opposite idea; its foundations are laid, its corner-stone rests, upon the great truth that the negro is not equal to the white man; that slavery subordination to the superior race is his natural and normal condition.[14]

Query: Does this speech articulate values compatible with American patriotism? Are they compatible with *our* values as an organization or community? Does Stephens' description of a government founded upon white supremacy, in opposition to the Constitution, allow for dual loyalty? Do the values expressed in the speech affirm or assault the dignity of our Black community members, customers, and neighbors?

This exercise uses questions to invite people to investigate their views instead of forcing them to fight in defense of them, in recognition of the fact that when you try to wrangle something away from someone, it prompts them to grip *harder*. Thus, this approach allows you to partner *with* people in a process of inquiry as opposed to setting yourself *against* them. In this spirit, one might probe: Is wearing a hat during the singing of the National Anthem unpatriotic? Why or why not? Is it unpatriotic to kneel during the national anthem to protest police brutality and its disproportionate impact upon people of color?[15] Why or why not? What values do such behaviors express? How compatible are those values with patriotism? Which is more offensive to American veterans and troops (including veterans and troop members of color) – not taking one's hat off during the national anthem, kneeling to protest police brutality and racial injustice during the national anthem, or celebrating those who fought *against* American troops for slavery in the Civil War? Why?

Judicious questions respectfully posed help people recognize inconsistencies and illogic in their thinking. Additionally, listening well and addressing the nuances in people's perspectives are, according to psychologists, keys to getting people to change their minds. The better you listen to people's answers, the more power to transform your questions will have.[16] The power of your questions also comes from the fact that they esteem those to whom they are directed because instead of the questioner treating those with whom he or she is speaking as reprobates to be looked down upon, the interrogator deals with his or her interlocutors as moral reasoners and appeals to the ethical authority located within their own articulations of values. Should those appeals fail, a leader may have to resort to putting his or her foot down and simply declaring that the organization or the community is not going to glorify white supremacy, but try to win over before defaulting to overruling.

There's a method to preparing yourself for intense conversation. Per Harvard Kennedy School Adjunct Lecturer Holly Weeks, before the conversation begins, reflect on what pushes your buttons – and unhelpful reactions you have to getting your buttons pushed.[17] For example, *When people act in a dismissive fashion, I tend to respond with sarcasm*. Once you take this into account, you can plan to respond better: *In this conversation, it is likely someone will behave dismissively, perhaps suggesting objections to the Confederate flag are just "political correctness stuff." When that happens, I'm not going to make a sarcastic remark – I'm going to continue to interact respectfully*.

Note that I said "unhelpful reactions" – not illegitimate ones. Your reactions to someone else's behavior may be justified – but that doesn't mean they'll help you achieve your goals.

Per Weeks, one way to restrain unhelpful reactions is to solicit the help of a neutral friend whose communication challenges aren't the same as yours. This person should be "a good listener, honest but nonjudgmental." First, tell the friend the message you want to convey without worrying about being impolitic. (Even a conversation such as this one that employs iterative questioning begins with prepared remarks.) Then, ask the friend to collaborate with you on writing out how you can convey the message in a refined tone. Write a script for yourself, so you can remember and practice how you plan to make your points – but don't read it during the real conversation! With your friend's help, continue to polish the way you say things. The trick to this process is that if you craft your language with a friend – instead of to an imagined adversary – your words become less aggressive. Finally, ask your friend to point out your body language when you convey the message, so you don't get undermined by your nonverbal communication.[18]

Priming for a fraught conversation is like getting ready for a school play – rehearse in front of an amicable audience to prepare yourself to take the stage.

Another strategy you could use in this situation is to remind your organization or community that the history we celebrate determines the history we create. For example, the cognitively dissonant belief that the Confederates who betrayed the United States were nevertheless patriotic Americans allowed for those attending the Save America Rally on January 6, 2020 to engage in an insurrection *against* the very nation they were purporting to rescue without perceiving any inconsistency – there's a reason one of the domestic terrorists carried the Confederate flag into the Capitol building during the coup.[19] Ask your community: What kind of history does celebrating the Confederacy create? What kind of history do we want to create? Are the two types of history in sync or in conflict?

Below are some other common arguments for celebrating white supremacy and techniques for responding.

If the argument is made that removing honors to those who committed crimes against humanity is a dystopian exercise akin to book burning, use the technique of historicizing, from Chapter 2, to offer context. For example, the year after World War II ended, the Allies issued Directive No. 20: Liquidation of German Military and Nazi Memorials and Museums.[20] If postwar Germany's denazification is not seen as objectionable, why should an analogous process be? If your interlocutors react defensively to their ancestors being equated with Nazis, engage in the questioning I described above to probe what distinguishes the two regimes morally in the minds of those offended by the comparison. Historicize, also, if someone argues that to remove a statute of a Confederate located on the grounds of your organization or in your community is to destroy art. The Society of Architectural Historians' Statement on the Removal of Monuments to the Confederacy from Public Spaces explains that Confederate monuments'

> existence can no longer be justified based on aesthetics, or their value as works of art or public sculpture. These monuments, especially the ones erected between the 1890s and the 1920s, are not so much objects of public art as proclamations of white supremacy rendered in granite and bronze.[21]

In other words, per the experts, Confederate monuments were no more meant to function as works of art than Klan hoods were to function as fashion statements, and we must stop trying to retroactively recategorize them. (If an organization or community *does*, in fact, have a commemorative object of artistic value, such as a painting of a Confederate general that happens to be by an acclaimed artist, then it belongs in a museum where it can be appreciated for its aesthetic and/or historic merit, not in a context where it holds moral authority as an artefact of community values. After all, the goal is not to erase history but to view it more honestly, to distinguish between memory and memorial, between what is, in fact, history and what is merely hagiography. Putting things in the appropriate physical place – such as a museum – can aid us in this taxonomic work.)

You may also hear a multicultural argument *for* honoring human rights abusers. For example, some Italian Americans have claimed that the removal of Columbus statues and opposition to Columbus Day are attacks on their heritage.[22] Point out this argument's solipsism as described in Chapter 2 – this claim forgets that the celebration of Columbus is an affront to the cultures he preyed upon. Also, underscore the double standard – Italian Americans, like white Southerners who honor the Confederate flag, make the claim that they are animated by "heritage, not hate." Yet their such assertions would not be considered valid if used by German Americans or Germans to attempt to justify the display of a statue or the celebration of a holiday honoring Adolph Hitler. Note that people are never all one thing – that one can be an explorer *and* an oppressor… just as one can be a statesman and an oppressor. We all need to understand that lest we fail to recognize current and future evildoers because they are more complex than we imagine them to be. The key is to weigh oppressors' gifts and sins against each other in the same fashion regardless of the color of their victims.

(And Columbus may not have even achieved the act for which he is heralded. For example, Garcilaso de la Vega, a mixed-race man of Incan and Spanish descent, described in his 1609 work *The Royal Commentaries of the Incas and General History of Peru* how a merchant named Alonso Sánchez de Huelva ended up in the Caribbean by accident. According to Garcilaso, upon returning to Spain in ill health, Alonso was cared for – and interrogated about his journey – by Columbus, who literally questioned the feeble man to death. In other words, it may be that Columbus wasn't so much good at "exploring" as he was at following directions.)[23]

And call out the double standard if you're told that we need monuments or memorials to white supremacists to remember history. Point out the fallacy of claiming, for example, that the United States needs monuments to Confederates to remember the Civil War, when it manages to remember the American Revolution without monuments to King George III, World War II without monuments to Hitler, and the Vietnam War without monuments to Ho Chi Minh.

Flag the double standard, as well, if someone argues, in the context of genocide against indigenous peoples, that "it's simply the way of the world for stronger populations to conquer weaker ones." The evil of the Holocaust is *never*, within the bounds of civil discourse, dismissed in those terms. Nor are white genocide victims disparaged as not having been strong or advanced enough to defend themselves against their exterminators. Rather than celebrating Nazis as being more powerful and modern than those they ethnically cleansed, we condemn them as having been more barbaric. Those who ethnically cleansed non-white people should be condemned the same.

Some try to distinguish between white supremacists, arguing that a man such as Jefferson Davis, President of the Confederacy, is revered *for* his sins, while a man like Thomas Jefferson is revered *despite* them. For example, journalist Philip Klein wrote in an op-ed that:

> In 2020, we do not celebrate Washington or Jefferson as slaveholders. We celebrate Washington as a general who led our struggle for independence and who was the first president. Somebody who had the clout and support to seize power for life but instead set the extraordinary example of giving up power after two terms in office and peacefully transferring it to a successor.... [I]f the standard becomes that we cannot honor those who did good because they also had flaws, then there's no way to establish any sort of shared history, especially as standards keep changing: Every few years, we'll have to start purging the past.[24]

In response to such sentiment, you could historicize by observing, for example, that Bernhard Lösener, a Nazi lawyer who subversively acted to limit the number of Jews subject to deportation to concentration camps, reminisced:

> If I may say so, I joined the [Nazi] Party not *because* of its Antisemitism, but – if I may put it this way – *despite* its Antisemitism, because I reassured myself with Hitler's promises that he would bring an end to the fighting and cure unemployment.[25]

Pointing to ideological precedent reveals the preposterousness of an ethos that requires us to dismiss antisemitism, slavery, and Native American genocide as picayune "flaws" and instead focus on the good Hitler, Washington, and Jefferson did or promised to do... for those who weren't unlucky enough to be their victims.

In rhetoric like Klein's, there are also double standards to reveal: Why should shared history mean sharing a view of perpetrators as worthy of celebration if their victims were not white yet condemnation if they were? Relatedly, why is viewing atrocity from the perspective of victims condemned as divisive when viewing it from the perspective of perpetrators is not, no matter how objectionable the latter view is to the populations harmed by perpetrators and others who condemn their deeds? (And why is "divisiveness" necessarily a pejorative when, for example, the abolition of slavery and women's suffrage were divisive?)

Arguments that echo Klein's claim that the "standards keep changing" also hail an appeal to the past: In the Nuremberg trials, in which Nazi leaders were prosecuted, defense counsel argued that it was improper for their clients to be tried for Crimes against Peace when, prior to the trial, such offenses didn't exist under international law.[26] The standards, they argued, had changed. The lawyers' protest – like Klein's op-ed – evoked the legal principle of *nullum crimen sine lege* or "no crime without law" meaning that one cannot be punished for an act that wasn't an offense before one performed it.

But as legal scholar, former member of the UN Human Rights Committee, and former member and Chairman of the UN International Law Commission Christian Tomuschat explains, the purpose of *nullum crimen* was to protect individuals from being punished for deeds they didn't realize were illegal. In contrast:

> ... crimes against humanity have deep roots in the minds of all human beings.... There cannot be the slightest doubt that all the offences set out under the title "crimes against humanity" are not only morally objectionable, but deserve to be punished and must be punished because of their abhorrent character if peaceful coexistence in human society is to be maintained. Nobody can legitimately claim that he believed that such actions in which he participated and that are to be classified as "crimes against humanity" were perfectly lawful.[27]

Similarly, the argument that it is unfair to "punish" Washington, Jefferson, or others who may be recognized as perpetrators of crimes against humanity in the future because the "standards keep changing" is morally null because the offenses for which these individuals are being "punished" have *always* been *inherently* detestable whether or not previously explicitly restricted by law or censured by public opinion.

But Klein also asserts something else: that not celebrating white supremacists is "purging the past." When you encounter an argument that not to celebrate a Washington or a Jefferson is an act of purgation, reframe: It's, in fact, celebrating a Washington requires purgation – we reach for the confetti with one hand and, with the other, shoo away the ghosts of the 317 slaves he owned at his death.[28] We fold up and hide away the note he wrote to his secretary describing his secret plan to keep his captives in his clutches: As historian Erica Armstrong Douglass explains:

> Once settled in Philadelphia, Washington encountered his first roadblock to slave ownership in the region – Pennsylvania's Gradual Abolition Act of 1780.... Under the law, any slave who entered Pennsylvania

with an owner and lived in the state for longer than six months would be set free automatically.

Washington developed a canny strategy that would protect his property and allow him to avoid public scrutiny. Every six months, the president's slaves would travel back to Mount Vernon or would journey with Mrs. Washington outside the boundaries of the state. In essence, the Washingtons reset the clock.[29]

We cover our ears, so we don't hear his order to his general that "[t]he immediate objects are the total destruction and devastation of [Iroquois Native Americans'] settlements and the capture of as many prisoners of every age and sex as possible," his command that Iroquois towns "not be merely overrun but destroyed."[30]

But when we stop *celebrating* Washington and start *studying* him, we broaden our gaze. We deepen our examination. We end up with *more* history – not less.

And in that more expansive history, we find people to celebrate – people like Ona Judge.

Ona Judge was only at the age of a college senior when she escaped from enslavement under George Washington.[31] Giving lie to Klein's praise of Washington for being a man willing to give up power, until Washington's death, he tried to trap Judge back in bondage.[32] She spent the following half century as a fugitive because, as a heritable good, after Washington's demise, until her own, she remained property. And yet, as an old woman, she risked recapture to speak out publicly against slavery.[33]

Isn't the history of someone with no power wrenching her freedom out of the grip of one of the most powerful families in the world worth celebrating? Isn't she a truer avatar of the American value of liberty than her captor? Just as we teach Adolf Hitler and Anne Frank in conjunction, we should teach George Washington and Ona Judge in conjunction. And we must point out that, ultimately, ceasing to celebrate perpetrators of genocide and slavery doesn't leave us destitute of history or bereft of the praiseworthy – it just means that instead of lauding perpetrators, we salute the people who struggled against, fought, or overcame them.

Welcoming a more expansive history means acknowledging that monsters may be graced with gifts. It means that we condemn monstrosity as unequivocally in those whose victims were non-white as we do in those whose victims were white – and that we make the strengths and accomplishments of those whose victims were white as much of a focus as those whose victims were not. By understanding how positives and negatives have been intertwined in the past, we can avoid making tradeoffs that amount to deals with the devil in the future.

And when engaging in conversations about white supremacist perpetrators, be mindful of the fact that many people don't recognize that their affinity for oppressors is a product of unconscious racism. So, calling someone who idolizes Columbus, Washington, or Jefferson a racist – even if accurate – is unlikely to be productive. Instead, engage in the questioning, listening, and other strategic communication skills discussed in this chapter to help people reach their own conclusions about why they excuse one group of perpetrators and denounce another.... As expressed earlier, the reason is the race of the perpetrators' victims. Engaging in this way can allow your interlocutor to experience the conversation as an empowering exercise in moral maturation rather than as an identity-wounding assault on his or her heroes and beliefs.

Now – let's talk more about whom we *should* celebrate.

On October 9, 2020, a portrait of Yale alumnus Dr. Edward Bouchet was unveiled on the campus of the University.[34] In 1876, Dr. Bouchet became the first Black person to earn a doctorate from an American university and one of the first half dozen of any race to earn a doctorate from an American university in physics.[35] And in 2021, he'll achieve another first – his will be the first portrait of a person of color to hang in the dining hall of Saybrook College, in the Yale residential college's near-century history.[36] Nor is Saybrook's racial homogeneity unique at Yale: fifty-five portraits hang in the Medical School – all of them of white people.[37]

Create a SMART plan (as described in Chapter 1) to remedy "whites only" commemoration. In terms of "M" for Measurability, if your organization or community acclaims historical figures regardless of whether they were affiliated with you, achieving population parity (domestically or globally) in commemorating people of different races may be an appropriate goal. On the other hand, if your organization or community primarily celebrates those who are part of its own history, but it didn't allow people of color to join until recently or they were or remain underrepresented, the goal could be to commemorate people in parity with its own demographics.

Who else might you salute? If your organization or community is located on the land of indigenous peoples who were dispossessed, you can acknowledge the traditional owners. Many institutions and communities celebrate their donors and founders yet forget that they are commonly the beneficiaries of people who had no choice about making what were often the most major contributions of them all. Those contributions can also be acknowledged verbally: In the United States, Native American events regularly start with what's called a land acknowledgment, a statement such as, "I'd like to begin by honoring the X People, the traditional owners of this land." But in Canada and Australia, land acknowledgments are part of mainstream culture, spoken by non-Natives even when no Natives are present. Consider adopting the practice.

In that same vein, if slaves are part of your organization's or community's history, or if they generated the wealth that donors and founders used to establish or support the institution – for example, Harvard Law was established with a bequest from Isaac Royall, Jr. of money generated by the slaves on his farms in Antigua and Massachusetts[38] – recognize that, too. You wouldn't give someone credit for plagiarized work, right? Question, then, why our society gives credit for gifts of "plagiarized" wealth? Cite your sources by following the example of Harvard Law School which installed a plaque on its premises that reads, "In honor of the enslaved whose labor created wealth that made possible the founding of Harvard Law School. May we pursue the highest ideals of law and justice in their memory."[39]

Such acts are examples of Vergangenheitsaufarbeitung, a term that, as scholar Susan Neiman explains in *Learning from the Germans: Race and the Memory of Evil*, means "working off the past." In Germany, the Nazi past is "worked off" by being constantly engaged – in movies, on television, in the classroom, at museums, through ubiquitous and/or prominent memorials, and during "public rites of repentance" commemorating specific events such as the Kristallnacht pogrom. Though you may not have the power to put "a monument to the Middle Passage or the genocide of Native Americans at the center of the Washington Mall" as Neiman suggests, she also muses, "Suppose you could walk down a New York street and step on a reminder that this building was constructed with slave labor." If your organization's building *was*, in fact, constructed with slave labor, get that marker installed![40]

Given that so many of our incomplete and false narratives about history are learned as children – and thus feel harder to relinquish – it is important Vergangenheitsaufarbeitung be part of how we teach the young. One way to do this is to teach subjects that call for Vergangenheitsaufarbeitung the way we do Holocaust history. For example, students could read *Incidents in the Life of a Slave Girl* the way they do the *Diary of Anne Frank*. Schools could invite survivors of atrocities such as lynching attempts (there were two in my family) and the Stolen Generation (indigenous Australian and Torres Strait Islander Children legally kidnapped from their families for generations, into the 1970s, for forcible assimilation) to speak at schools as they do Holocaust survivors. Schools could take trips to the National Memorial for Peace and Justice which is dedicated to victims of slavery, lynching and racial terror, apartheid, and discrimination in the criminal justice system as they do to the United States Holocaust Memorial Museum.

(I would be remiss, however, not to note how the ethos of Vergangenheitsaufarbeitung contrasts with Germany's attitude toward other parts of its past. The first genocide of the twentieth century was the Herero and Nama Genocide in which Germany sought to exterminate the two African ethnic groups indigenous to its colony in what is now Namibia and succeeded in killing off eighty percent of the Herero and fifty percent of the Nama.[41] In contrast to the Holocaust, which the world is exhorted to "never forget," the Herero and Namaqua Genocide is referred to as "the forgotten genocide." As of 2012, the sixtieth year of German governmental reparations, the country had paid $89 billion in reparations to Holocaust victims.[42]

It has refused to even *consider* paying reparations to the Herero and Nama.[43]

Furthermore, even though the goal of Vergangenheitsaufarbeitung is to work off the Nazi past, non-white victims of that past have largely been ignored. Roma and Sinti peoples (who are so oppressed that they are better recognized by the racial slur "g★psy") have become known as the forgotten victims of the Holocaust despite the fact that between a fourth and a half of their population was exterminated in it.[44]

Most Roma and Sinti survivors and their descendants have not received *any* reparations).[45]

But let's return from this depressing digression.

So, people of color should be celebrated and their suffering memorialized, but do you know what else is key? Applauding good white people. As a little girl, I constantly heard teachers defend, for example, George Washington's slave ownership with the excuse that he was "a man of his era" and shouldn't be condemned because "everyone felt that way back then." As a child, I'd mentally retort that I was pretty sure Washington's *slaves* hadn't felt that way back then. What my teachers meant, of course, was that all *white* people felt that way back then.

And even on that account, they were wrong.

People cannot be exculpated by the excuse that they were men and women of their time. Rather, it must be recognized that they were men and women *of their choices*. When we celebrate historical white antiracists, we show that there always is and *always has been* a choice between right and wrong. And we offer *true* white heroes to venerate… and emulate.

For example, Yale celebrates Roger Sherman Baldwin, a white attorney alumnus who argued the *Amistad* case, defending slaves who had led a successful insurrection onboard the eponymous slave ship against those who wanted to re-enslave them. (Matthew McConaughey plays him in the movie.) *Some* nineteenth-century lawyers (cough – Abraham Lincoln – cough) had no qualms about arguing the opposite side of re-enslavement cases (cough – *Matson v. Rutherford* – cough), but others chose differently. The contrast between Baldwin's and Lincoln's legal practices shows that though we don't get to choose *when* we live, we *do* get to choose *how*.

That said, don't go to the *other* extreme and whitewash history. For example, in contradictory fashion, though we are told that, on the one hand, slaveholders shouldn't be denounced because "everyone felt that way by then," on the other hand, the abolitionist movement is commonly portrayed as white. The first notion erases whites' autonomy; the second erases the core role Blacks played in their own liberation. (It also ignores the support they got from other peoples of color.) Whites like Baldwin were heroes – not saviors.

A few more things to remember about celebrating the past: First, don't just commemorate people of color for race-related accomplishments – doing so implies that while white people contribute to humanity in every domain, non-whites' achievements are limited to their struggles against racism. Bring to light, for example, how the U.S. government was inspired by Iroquois

Native American government, which is one of the world's oldest democracies, or how a slave named Onesimus helped introduce the traditional African medical practice of inoculation to the West. Second, don't pigeonhole non-white races: For example, the Native Americans most non-Natives know – Tisquantum (Squanto), Amonute (commonly known by non-Native Americans by her nickname "Pocahontas"), Sacagawea, Geronimo, Tȟašúŋke Witkó (His Horse Is Crazy, commonly known by non-Lakota Native Americans as "Crazy Horse"), and Tȟatȟáŋka Íyotake (Sitting Bull) all lived – or were primarily active – before the twentieth century and are all defined by their relationship to colonialism. Celebrating individuals like Maria Tallchief of the Osage tribal nation who was one of the most important ballerinas of the twentieth century helps reflect the diversity of the Native American experience and reminds that American Indians continued (and continue) to exist beyond the era of the "Wild West." And third, make sure you're celebrating history and not mythology – Rosa Parks did not refuse to give up her seat on the bus to a white passenger because her feet were tired! She was a seasoned activist who had attended an actual activism school: the still operating Highlander Research and Education Center (formerly Highlander Folk School). The event that inspired the Montgomery Bus Boycott wasn't even the first time she'd refused to give up her seat. And Hamilton was not an abolitionist; he was a slave trader.[46]

Here, you might be thinking, *"Onesimus?" "Maria Tallchief?" I've never heard of these people.* How can you diversify your celebration of the past when it means incorporating history you were never taught? One trick is to see what books are on the syllabi of relevant courses at top universities – such syllabi are commonly publicly available online. Look also to the catalogs of those universities' presses. Some universities even produce materials for children such as Harvard University's Hutchins Center for African & African American Research's *Selma Online* curriculum. Additionally, human rights organizations such as Equal Justice Initiative and cultural institutions such as the Smithsonian's National Museum of the American Indian offer quality educational resources – including for children – often for free. And when it comes to how to teach and learn history in an antiracist fashion, acclaimed historian James W. Loewen literally wrote the book on it: *Teaching What Really Happened: How to Avoid the Tyranny of Textbooks & Get Students Excited About Doing History*. Others of Loewen's works focus on everything from Columbus to sundown towns (communities that excluded non-whites, including through signs warning that the presence of people of color was not permitted after dark). And his antiracist classic *Lies My Teacher Told Me: Everything Your American History Textbook Got Wrong* is available in editions for both adults and children.

Let's talk about race-related holidays, next. Some holidays such as Columbus Day or Jefferson Davis' birthday glorify white supremacists. There are a couple of ways to approach these. Take Columbus Day, for instance. Some organizations and communities choose not to acknowledge it at all, while others observe the counter-holiday that occurs on the same date – Indigenous Peoples' Day – which celebrates not Columbus but the Native nations who survived his impact. Both choices are ethical. We *should* learn about Columbus and his complexities – just as we should learn about Hitler and his – but, like anyone who exterminated people, he should not be *celebrated*, so the day on which we learn about him should not be a *holiday*.

(Instead of observing a holiday dedicated to Columbus, students could spend a day studying Garcilaso's account of him, the letter from one of Columbus' men in which he describes how the girl Columbus gave him as a sex slave "made unheard of cries which you wouldn't have believed" as he raped her,[47] and Columbus' policy of chopping off the hands of indigenous people over the age of fourteen who did not provide him with sufficient gold.[48] They could also study his talents as a cartographer and marine pilot. Such would be a manifestation of the ethos of learning more history rather than less and provide an occasion to reckon with and reflect upon human complexity.)

In practice, though, many peoples' "observance" of either Columbus Day or Indigenous Peoples' Day consists merely of not attending work or school. Thus, converting the former holiday into the latter can render it inoffensive yet leave it substantively meaningless. So, consider celebrating honorable race-related holidays such as Indigenous Peoples' Day with a "day on" rather than a "day off." For example, in 2020, Facebook marked Juneteenth, the American holiday marking the end of slavery, by having employees come *into* the office… to learn about racism.[49] A day *on* doesn't have to mean a day *in* work or school, though – think of it instead as a day spent "on topic" whether at the office, in the classroom, or in the community. Days on can also occur during one day of a cultural history month such as Black History Month or Hispanic Heritage Month.

Note that Facebook's antiracist "day on" actually related to antiracism. You'd think that would be a given, but, in fact, it's not. For example, journalist Rick Cohen observed that Martin Luther King, Jr. Day was promoted on a national government website as MLK National Day of Service – but the website recommended performing volunteer service that had nothing to do with civil rights such as gardening at the National Arboretum and helping at the National Oceanic and Atmospheric Administration. Those are worthy causes, but as Cohen pointed out, Martin Luther King, Jr. Day should not merely be a general "Day of Service" but a "day of fighting racial injustice."[50] When *your* organization or community is planning a day on, heed Cohen's critique and make the revelry relevant.

What can your organization or community do on a day on? Learn, act, or both. For example, on Martin Luther King, Jr. Day, a law firm could hold a seminar in a Black community teaching legal scholar Paul Butler's strategy for using jury nullification to fight discriminatory prosecution, while a public relations firm might spend a day advising an environmental justice group on how to raise awareness about a new toxic site being slotted for a Black neighborhood that already bears more than its fair share of ecological burdens. Or a community or well-resourced organization could put on a free symposium, open to the public, on little-known issues that affect African Americans such as racial disparities in amputation (Black patients are three times more likely to undergo diabetic amputations than non-Black patients, even though their amputations are often preventable)[51] and wrongful conviction (Blacks are thirteen percent of the U.S. population yet almost *half* of those exonerated for being wrongfully convicted).[52] On Indigenous Peoples' Day, a Native American-owned and -operated business might bring in a traditional artist to introduce employees to a craft such as beadworking as a means of revitalizing a cultural tradition, while a non-Native American company could screen a documentary about a social issue affecting indigenous peoples that outsiders know little about, such as the epidemic of Missing and Murdered Indigenous Women, and spend the rest of the day at a Native American museum learning about the forces of colonialism, past and present, that render Native women vulnerable.

Beyond holidays, find creative ways to weave the past into present. Even if you don't have the resources to *wow* people by unveiling a grand monument to someone like Charles Hamilton Houston, you *do* have the power to *woo* them into learning history through small yet thoughtful gestures. If your organization – be it a hair salon or a doctor's office – has a waiting room, why not place works with catchy titles, such as Noel Ignatiev's nonfiction adult book *How the Irish Became White*, or irresistible covers such as the fictional picture book *We Are Water Protectors* by Carole Lindstrom, which is inspired by twenty-first-century indigenous environmental activism against dangerous oil pipelines, among the fashion and golf magazines? Why not keep kids occupied while they wait for their meals at your restaurant with crayons and pages from Civil Rights-themed coloring books (the kind that have historical fact captions) as well as other creative materials such as civil rights leader and congressman John Lewis' graphic novel? Whatever your domain, find a way to act as an agent of memory.

But *recalling* the past is one thing – *rectifying* it is another. Here's a step-by-step guide for doing so.

Step one: Reckon with past internal racism.

Review the institutional internal workings of your organization or community, as described in Chapter 3, as retroactively as you are able. If internal racism is identified, first acknowledge, then apologize, and then act.

For example, if your institution, until recent decades, would only hire people of color as janitorial or secretarial staff, recognize that by denying non-whites access to higher paying jobs, you contributed to the wealth gap (described in Chapter 3), and even if, going forward, you bring on non-whites in higher paying roles in parity with their presence in the population, that doesn't change the fact that their communities still financially lag behind those who've had disproportionate access to such opportunities all along. In such a case, acting could mean helping people of color grow their capital by investing in minority-owned businesses or partnering with an organization like Prosperity Now that engages in projects, research, and advocacy to help people of color and low-income people of all races produce wealth.

Ultimately, both remorse and remedy are key. The latter helps make things right; the former helps make them *real*. Too often, people think of systemic racism as abstract or theoretical. But when organizations and communities offer a full and public accounting of perpetrating it and explain the consequences of having done so, the public recognizes systemic racism as a real force perpetrated by real entities with real effects on real people.

Step two: Reckon with atonement and/or reparations and work off the past.

Audit your organization or community's history to uncover and elucidate instances of harming or directly benefitting from the harm of people of color. Members of the Universities Studying Slavery Consortium, consisting of nearly eighty schools throughout the United States and in Canada and Europe, are engaging in a process of "research, acknowledgement, and atonement."[53] Princeton Theological Seminary conducted a two-year audit of its involvement with slavery,[54] and Memorial Episcopal Church examined its participation in both slavery and segregation.[55] The Episcopal Diocese of Maryland formed a Truth and Reconciliation Commission to research the slavery in its diocese and its impact.[56] Its fellow Diocese of New York created a committee to gather and record evidence of its complicity in slavery, segregation, and discrimination.[57]

Your own audit should not be narrowly targeted to a specific form of injustice but should be comprehensive. There are resources available to aid in such investigations. For example, the Legacies of British Slave-ownership database and the Dictionary of British Slave Traders (forthcoming) trace the slave-wealth of organizations/communities, the individuals who funded them, and the assets purchased by such funds, and the Morrill Act of 1862 Indigenous Land Parcels Database identifies parcels of land violently seized from indigenous nations. (Historians and other professionals can be of help, too.)[58] But be mindful that not all racial injustices are linked to high-profile atrocities. For example, an audit may find that yours was one of the insurance companies that refused to compensate victims of the Tulsa race massacre for their property losses[59] or that the reason your organization was able to snap up cheap land in a gentrifying community of color was because the property values had been wracked by redlining (the practice of denying credit and disinvesting in minority neighborhoods).

If your organization or community perpetrated or directly profited from the harm of people of color, then, as in Step one, both apology and atonement/reparations are imperative. I speak of both atonement and reparations because some injustices, though grave, are of a scale that allows organizations and communities to speak properly of "reparations." Others, however, are not.

For example, Duke University economist William Darity warns that in the case of American slavery, even when private institutions were perpetrators or direct beneficiaries, the participation of the federal government is required for justice to be done to the most complete extent possible. This contrasts with the independent and ad hoc, even if admirable, efforts at making reparations for African American slavery that I will describe below, efforts in which organizations and communities unilaterally determine what justice for victims and their descendants look like. "Atonement" is Darity's word for such initiatives.[60]

Darity affirms that atonement is "essential,"[61] but he also calls upon organizations to lobby for a federal reparations plan for slavery and the injustice that followed.[62] This two-pronged process has precedent in reckoning with Holocaust history: For example, Holocaust reparations were – and are still – paid by the German government. But also, the German government and other European governments, the United States, and Israel joined with German industry to create the Foundation Remembrance, Responsibility, and Future that made and makes reparation to victims of Nazism and the populations it targeted, including those who performed forced labor for private corporations.[63] The International Commission on Holocaust Era Insurance Claims, which settled Holocaust era insurance claims, was created after negotiations with European insurance companies, Jewish and Holocaust survivor organizations, U.S. insurance regulators, and Israel.[64] The U.S. Senate Banking Committee held hearings on Holocaust Era Assets held in Swiss banks owed to Nazi victims and descendants,[65] and the U.S. Office of the Special Envoy for Holocaust Issues has helped secure reparations for victims and descendants from private entities.[66] All these examples show the role of national governments (particularly the government that made the horror legal) in providing reparations to victims of private entities.

However, acts of atonement occur beyond the aforementioned contexts. For example, the Reimann family, which controls JAB Holding Company, which supported the Nazis and used forced labor, donated five million euros to a fund that aids Holocaust survivors and is using another five million to locate and donate to those who performed forced labor at JAB's predecessor company.[67] Thus, we see the German government paid Holocaust reparations, and Germany as well as other national governments have worked with private organizations to make reparations to the organizations' Nazi-era victims, but independent efforts toward redress for perpetrating or directly benefitting from Nazi-era crimes are also made.

Below are further precedents for atonement:

- Princeton Theological Seminary created a twenty-component program including scholarships for descendants of slaves and members of underrepresented groups and investment in community partnerships,[68] dedicating 2.25 percent of its endowment to the effort.[69]

- Virginia Theological Seminary is spending income from a special endowment (that represents 1.1 percent of its total endowment)[70] making what it refers to as reparations to the descendants of slaves who worked on its campus and of African Americans employed there during segregation. (It has hired historians and genealogists to locate them.) It is also supporting the work of African American alumni, investing in the development of African American clergy, supporting efforts toward "justice and inclusion," and mobilizing for governmental reparations. The school acknowledges that such initiatives are but a *"start."*[71]
- Memorial Episcopal Church, which was involved in slavery, segregation, redlining, Black voter disenfranchisement, and inequitable school and youth programs, plans to spend $500,000 combating racial inequality through Black-led initiatives.[72] The initial $50,000 withdrawn from the Church's coffers is ten percent of the parish's endowment.[73] Another $50,000 was drawn from the operating budget. It will fundraise the remaining money.[74]
- The Diocese of Maryland, upon finding that most, if not all, of its pre-1860 churches were built by slaves or by the fiscal beneficiaries of slave labor as well as that it played a large role in redlining and even built a cathedral to serve parishioners participating in white flight from what, in its historical documents, was referred to as a Black "invasion," will use one-fifth of its operating budget on "reparations" it expects to take the form of funding programs benefitting Black entrepreneurs, students, and nursing home residents.[75]
- Private organizations (as well as the U.S. federal government and at least one U.S. municipality) have returned land to the indigenous peoples from whom it was dispossessed.[76] Additionally, Californian indigenous peoples have established the Sogorea Te' Land Trust to reacquire their homelands, and non-indigenous denizens of those homelands can pay the trust a voluntary "tax" to be used as capital toward that end.[77] Although it is preferable to return wrongfully seized property outright, and there is precedent for such return in, for example, the restitution of Holocaust Era Assets and looted art to Nazi victims and descendants, paying a voluntary tax is a *beginning* step. Organizations and communities should look for similar programs in their own locales. They should also lobby national governments of countries that ethnically cleansed and/or subjugated indigenous people for reparations for those populations.

Legal remedies can also offer guidance on atonement and reparation. Even when an organization or community is attempting to right wrongs out of a sense of moral responsibility – rather than being forced into doing so by litigation – considering various legal remedies offers ways of conceptualizing what justice requires: For example, compensatory damages reimburse for harm – including for the ripple effects of a wrong and for suffering. Punitive damages go beyond reimbursement and grant further monies to the wronged party to punish a wrongdoer's particularly abhorrent behavior. Constructive trust transfers wrongfully procured or retained property to its rightful owner. Disgorgement returns the profits or gains of wrongdoing to the harmed party. And abatement can reimburse for the costs of correcting the wrongful interference of enjoyment of property or harming the wellbeing of a community. Note that courts commonly find that multiple remedies are appropriate.

Many of the entities whose atonement I described also engage in Vergangenheitsaufarbeitung:

- Princeton Theological Seminary is educating all community members about the history of slavery at the school and naming buildings after African American community members such as Betsey Stockton, a former slave owned by a chair of the Seminary's Board of Trustees who became a noted educator and missionary.[78]
- Virginia Theological Seminary is working with the descendants of slaves and segregation-era employees who worked at the school to determine how to memorialize their ascendants and share their history.[79]
- Memorial Episcopal Church details its involvement with slavery on its website. Community members visited the plantation owner whom *Memorial* Episcopal Church memorializes to learn, repent, and perform a ritual of "sanctification." It further decided that the Church will no longer memorialize that slave owner and has invited members of its community to help decide what the Church will memorialize instead. The Church removed and deconsecrated plaques honoring slave owners from its garden and commissioned an artist to create a memorial for the slaves of the Church's founding rectors. Members of the Church community who descended from those enslaved by the family of the Church's founders shared their stories with the community. Additionally, the Church engaged its past through study, discussions, sermons, liturgies, retreats, community events, and ceremonies and plans to proceed with a study of "Gospel Centered Justice."[80]
- The Episcopal Churches of Maryland hosts an annual pilgrimage to sites linked to slavery, and the Episcopal Church and will support government reparations.[81]
- The Diocese of New York of the Episcopal Church, while in the process of planning how to use 2.5 percent of its endowment on making amends for its church and its leaders' ownership of slaves, its use of slave labor and slave-wealth, its rejection of antebellum resolutions condemning slavery,[82] and for the de jure and systemic racism resulting from the institution, engaged in plethora of Vergangenheitsaufarbeitung activities. These included adopting the rejected resolutions; making a DVD about the Episcopal Church's role in the slave trade and ties to segregation and racism as well as the legacies of those oppressions; developing an

ecclesiastical resource on reparations; resolving to make a formal apology for slavery; placing plaques on the buildings of parishes whose first or current buildings were built by slave labor or slave-wealth; engaging in a Year of Lamentations for the Diocese's role in slavery with events including theatrical presentations, liturgies, book and film discussions, workshops, and trips to historical sites; and resolving to participate in continued public Diocesan conversations about reparations with the long-term goal of changing orthopraxis.[83]

Note the faith-based organizations that frame their efforts in spiritual terms such as "repentance" and "lamentation" and include theology in their Vergangenheitsaufarbeitung efforts. All organizations and communities can learn from their example – use language, matrices, and authorities that resonate with *your* people to build support. A church with an elderly congregation may be confused or annoyed by calls to atone for and work off the past that employ the latest social justice slang, while a secular corporation might be unimpressed with or offended by a call to atonement that appeals to scriptural authority.

Step three: Reckon with the history of systemic racism on fields and by fields.

Past systemic racism bedevils present-day fields. For example, many states prevent ex-convicts from participating in legal marijuana commerce,[84] but Blacks were *nearly four times* more likely than whites to be arrested for marijuana-related crimes despite the fact that both races committed such crimes at the same rate.[85] Thus, laws banned marijuana usage and sales, used that ban to criminalize Blacks, and then turned around and legalized/decriminalized marijuana usage and sales, creating an industry that you can only profit from if you weren't convicted under the old regime – a $18 billion industry[86] that favors whites by getting rid of much of their would-be competition.

When a field has been twisted by systemic racism, antiracist stakeholders within it act both to halt those systems and to remedy their effects by researching, innovating, and implementing solutions in concert with the harmed communities. The Minority Cannabis Business Association and Minorities 4 Medical Marijuana (M4MM) proffer many such solutions for their own field from white-owned cannabis businesses helping minority-owned businesses reduce their startup expenses by sharing resources such as legal or marketing teams or office space with them to cannabis industry participants lobbying for equity in cannabis legalization,[87] perhaps for laws such as Portland, Oregon's local retail cannabis sales tax, part of which "supports record clearing, workforce reentry, and cannabis small business support, with a specific focus on helping communities that have been most impacted by cannabis prohibition."[88]

But fields aren't just shaped *by* systemic racism – sometimes they *are* the system. Legal scholar Mary Szto describes how the real estate industry engaged in discriminatory practices such as redlining, reverse redlining (targeting people in redlined neighborhoods for predatory lending), and racial steering (guiding home buyers to or away from neighborhoods based on the buyers' race, often to perpetuate de facto segregation) and offers suggestions for how they can right those wrongs.[89] Those suggestions can be extrapolated to other industries. For example, her encouragement to "[d]evelop training materials that describe the history of the realty industry in redlining and reverse red lining" and to "[c]onduct intensive training on methods to avoid steering and other present day discriminatory practices with appropriate disciplinary methods for noncompliance" can be generalized to training workers on the history of discrimination in their field and on how to avoid practicing systemic racism – and then holding them accountable.

- "Develop[ing] consumer education on these practices as well" can be expanded to a precept of educating the public on the institutional racism in one's field.
- "Developing compensation incentives for greenlining" – the practice of investing redlined communities – and "[c]ontribut[ing] to organizations that promote greenlining and community development" are synecdoches for engaging in, rewarding, and funding practices and efforts that counter an industry's racial transgressions.
- Her directive to national and to racial and ethnic real estate affinity groups to join as a task force to address racism in the industry can be abstracted to urging major stakeholders to partner with members of harmed communities to right racist wrongs.
- The counsel to "[l]obby legislatures for tax incentives and continuing education requirements for the above" can be generalized to advice to invest one's resources in relevant, antiracist policy solutions – preferably ones that offer concrete rewards for good behavior, and, I'd add, concrete, *enforced* consequences for bad behavior and a mechanism for ensuring compliance.[90]

Among these suggestions, I would also insert that organizations should lobby to make education on the history of racism in a field and how to avoid practicing it part of the credentialing process, and, in the case of forms of systemic racism that play a significant role in racial disparities, part of public-school curricula.

Finally, as described in Chapter 1, don't be colormum. Talk about and demystify the impact of racism on your field or of your field's racism on society (or both) in conversations with other stakeholders and with the public, and make sure all the members of your organization or community understand it as well.

For example, Szto suggests real estate brokers and their organizations "[a]dopt a letter of hope and healing" that plainly and candidly states:

> …. we [as a field] have promoted or enabled segregated communities through racial covenants, blockbusting, steering, and reverse redlining

and promotion of subprime mortgages. These segregated communities have enabled predatory lending and racial profiling, and fostered vast disparities in access to education, credit, transportation, work, nutrition, and intergenerational wealth transfer....[91]

Step four: Reckon with the legacy of racism and imperialism in the places where you serve.

Engage in deep study of the racial history of the communities you aid. Integrate truth-telling, decolonizing, cultural revitalizing, and antiracist efforts into solutions to problems faced by non-Western and non-white populations. Make rectifying the legacy of imperialism and racism, including through truth and reconciliation, atonement, and reparation on the part of both public and private entities, a focus of social initiatives and philanthropic efforts.

Here's how that can look in practice:

Biopiracy is the intellectual property theft of traditional ecological knowledge such as plant strains cultivated by indigenous botanists or ethno-pharmacological knowledge. Contrary to the stereotype of the uneducated non-Western woman, this knowledge is commonly the product of female scientific expertise.[92] Over two decades ago, it was calculated that if intellectual property royalties were paid for biopirated knowledge, the United States would owe "Third World" countries $5.1 billion a year for pharmaceuticals and an additional $302 billion a year for agricultural products[93] – and since then, the thieving has continued. Thus, a nonprofit or church might decide that instead of sponsoring an aid worker or missionary to help women in a foreign country start a co-op, it might sponsor a lawyer to fight for the intellectual property rights of and the restitution of royalties to victimized peoples. That would be an example of using decolonizing and antiracist efforts to address what, on its surface, appears to be a problem of poverty but is, at its root, a problem of racial injustice.

The truth-telling component of such an effort involves being honest and forthcoming within organizations and communities and vis-à-vis those they serve, donors, other stakeholders, and the public about the provenance of the problems we seek to remedy. And it encompasses rejecting language that disguises that provenance, of choosing to speak, perhaps, of "restitution" instead of "charity," "rebuilding" instead of "development," or "repentance trips" instead of "mission trips."

Here's another example: Consider the situation of the Black community of Portland, Oregon. Until the 1970s, because of racist lending practices, such as those supported by the city's Realty Board's Code of Ethics' ban on realtors selling minorities properties in white neighborhoods and on bankers loaning them money to purchase such properties, the neighborhood of Albina was one of the few in which Black Portlanders could buy homes. But in the 1970s, Portland seized Albina's land to expand a health facility called Emmanuel Hospital without making promised compensation to landowners.[94]

A nonprofit that has not reckoned with the legacy of racism might encourage the city to support the plundered Black Portland community by building more affordable rental housing, something that, as of writing, Portland's city council is indeed considering. But a nonprofit that *has* so reckoned might take – or support – the actions of the Oregon Law Center and Legal Aid Services of Oregon of advocating for the Emanuel Displaced Persons Association 2 as they seek compensation for their lost homes, businesses, and business revenue.[95] In other words, they would realize that the root of the problem is not poverty but historical racial injustice, and thus, the solution is not charity but racial justice.

Step five: Reckon with how the past affects and *infects* the present.

The past isn't a story with a conclusion – it's a story with consequences. Study that story and seek out ways you can use your resources to mitigate the negative ones. For example, Black-owned businesses are more vulnerable to the negative economic effects of the coronavirus pandemic than their white-owned counterparts because of the plethora of ways systemic racism affects them, from the reality that, because of the wealth gap, Black entrepreneurs have less resources to support their businesses in hard times to the fact that when the federal government created a Paycheck Protection Program that funded banks to aid small businesses with the expenses of employee salaries and benefits and rent and mortgage interest, banks that serviced Black communities were excluded from the first round of funding.[96] In other words, an ongoing history of racial injustice renders Black entrepreneurs particularly vulnerable in the present. But Discover credit card company stepped up and decided to give $5 million dollars to Black-owned restaurants during the coronavirus pandemic.[97] Additionally, Verizon, which is not in the field of finance but telecommunications, started a $7.5 million grant program for American small businesses focusing on entrepreneurs who are female, of color, or from other communities that have been underserved historically.[98] The latter is an example of antiracist thinking that goes beyond asking, "What are the wrongs in my realm that my resources could address?" to "What are the wrongs that could be addressed by my resources… in any realm?"

Also important, explain *why* you're doing what you're doing. If you don't, some people will think your organization or community is engaging in reverse racism. Your explanation will enlighten those who aren't aware of how the injustices of the past act as puppeteer to the present.

Step six: Repeat Steps one through five.

There's always more about the past to learn and still more being uncovered. As of this writing, scholar Jonathan Daniel Wells just released a book on the role of Wall Street in the slave trade, scholar Steven Press just released a book connecting the German diamond trade to the genocide of the Herero and Nama, and investigators at *High Country News* recently published a feature about how eleven million acres of land were violently taken from Native American nations to endow fifty-two American land-grant universities and how the atrocity continues to enrich them to this day.[99] And those efforts represent just a sampling of the information continually being generated about our racial past. That information often implicates our fields and even our specific organizations and communities.

Many industries have continuing education requirements borne of the understanding that individuals who work in those industries must continually refresh their skills and update their knowledge. Antiracist organizations and communities must recognize the ongoing duty to keep themselves apprised of news of the past, because our visions of tomorrow are contingent upon our retrospection and our action. As antiracists, we long for the realization of Martin Luther King, Jr.'s dream. But we can't make that dream of the future come true until we reckon with the nightmares of the past.

Notes

1 Jennifer L. Morgan, *Laboring Women: Reproduction and Gender in New World Slavery* (Philadelphia: University of Pennsylvania Press, 2004), 140; Ned Sublette and Constance Sublette, *American Slave Coast: A History of the Slave-Breeding Industry* (Chicago, IL: Lawrence Hill Press, 2016), 22; Susan Neiman, *Learning from the Germans: Race and the Memory of Evil* (New York: Farrar, Straus, and Giroux, 2019), 32.
2 Greg Satell, "4 Tips for Managing Organizational Change," *Harvard Business Review*, March 24, 2021, https://hbr.org/2019/08/4-tips-for-managing-organizational-change.
3 Ibid.
4 "The Diocesan Reparations Committee," The Episcopal Diocese of New York, February 13, 2021, https://www.dioceseny.org/mission-and-outreach/social-concerns/reparations-for-slavery/.
5 Matthew J. Cressler and Adelle M. Banks, "Reparations and Religion: 50 Years after 'Black manifesto'," *ABC News*, December 30, 2019, https://abcnews.go.com/US/wireStory/reparations-religion-50-years-black-manifesto-67989717; "Knee on My Neck: Slavery's Ghost: A Study of the Persistent Underlying Principles of Racist Policies," *Roots & Branches*, March 24, 2021, https://rootsandbranchesprograms.org/knee-on-my-neck/.
6 Satell, "Tips."
7 Ibid.
8 "100 Law Firms Announced as Mansfield Rule 3.0 Certified," *Mansfield Rule: Boosting Diversity in Leadership*, Diversity Lab, March 24, 2021, https://www.diversitylab.com/pilot-projects/mansfield-rule-3-0/.
9 Satell, "Tips."
10 Mark Osborne, "Trump Weighs in on Tearing down Columbus Statues: 'What's Next? Has to Be 'Stopped'," *ABC News*, October 18, 2017, https://abcnews.go.com/Politics/trump-weighs-tearing-columbus-statues-whats-stopped/story?id=50553722.
11 James W. Loewen, *Lies My Teacher Told Me: Everything Your American History Textbook Got Wrong* (New York: Simon & Schuster, 1995), 60, 63.
12 John M. Coski, *The Confederate Battle Flag: America's Most Embattled Emblem* (Cambridge, MA: Belknap Press, 2005), 294.
13 Robert Draper, "Toppling Statues is a First Step toward Ending Confederate Myths," *National Geographic*, July 2, 2020, https://www.nationalgeographic.com/history/2020/07/toppling-statues-is-first-step-toward-ending-confederate-myths/.

14 "Cornerstone Speech," *Civil War*, American Battlefield Trust, January 21, 2021, https://www.battlefields.org/learn/primary-sources/cornerstone-speech.
15 Frank Edwards, Hedwig Lee, and Michael Esposito, "Risk of Being Killed by Police Use-of-Force in the U.S. by Age, Race/Ethnicity, and Sex," *Proceedings of the National Academy of Sciences*. https://www.pnas.org/cgi/doi/10.1073/pnas.1821204116.
16 Adam Grant, "The Science of Reasoning with Unreasonable People," *New York Times*, January 31, 2020, https://www.nytimes.com/2021/01/31/opinion/change-someones-mind.html.
17 Holly Weeks, "Taking the Stress Out of Stressful Conversations," *Harvard Business Review*, July–August 2001, https://hbr.org/2001/07/taking-the-stress-out-of-stressful-conversations.
18 Ibid.
19 Jordan Brasher, "The Confederate Battle Flag, Which Rioters Flew Inside the US Capitol, Has Long Been a Symbol of White Insurrection," *The Conversation*, January 14, 2020, https://theconversation.com/the-confederate-battle-flag-which-rioters-flew-inside-the-us-capitol-has-long-been-a-symbol-of-white-insurrection-153071.
20 "Enactments and Approved Papers of the Control Council and Coordinating Committee – law-index," Library of Congress, February 15, 2021, https://www.loc.gov/rr/frd/Military_Law/Enactments/03LAW28.pdf#[5,{%22name%22:%22FitH%22.
21 "SAH Statement on The Removal of Monuments to the Confederacy from Public Spaces," Society of Architectural Historians, last modified June 19, 2020, https://www.sah.org/about-sah/news/sah-news/news-detail/2020/06/19/sah-statement-on-the-removal-of-monuments-to-the-confederacy-from-public-spaces.
22 Mathew Impelli, "Italian Americans Have a Columbus Conundrum," *Newsweek*, June 18, 2020, https://www.newsweek.com/italian-americans-have-columbus-conundrum-1511262.
23 Doris Sommer, *Proceed with Caution, When Engaged by Minority Writing in the Americas* (Cambridge, MA: Harvard University Press, 1999), 74–75.
24 Philip Klein, "Now, They're Coming for George Washington and Thomas Jefferson," *Washington Examiner*, June 19, 2020, https://www.washingtonexaminer.com/opinion/now-theyre-coming-for-george-washington-and-thomas-jefferson.
25 David Luban, "Complicity and Lesser Evils: A Tale of Two Lawyers" (paper, International Nuremberg Principles Academy, Nuremberg, Germany, September 27–28, 2019).
26 "Motion Adopted by All Defense Counsel (★)," *Nuremberg Trial Proceedings Vol. 1*, Lillian Goldman Law Library, January 16, 2021, https://avalon.law.yale.edu/imt/v1-30.asp#1.
27 Christian Tomuschat, "The Legacy of Nuremberg," *Journal of International Criminal Justice* 4 (2006): 835, https://doi.org/10.1093/jicj/mql051.
28 Robert F. Dalzell and Lee Baldwin Dalzell, *George Washington's Mount Vernon at Home in Revolutionary America* (New York: Oxford University Press, 1998), 130.
29 Erica Armstrong Dunbar, "George Washington, Slave Catcher," *New York Times*, February 16, 2015, https://www.nytimes.com/2015/02/16/opinion/george-washington-slave-catcher.html.
30 Colin G. Calloway, *The Indian World of George Washington: The First President, the First Americans, and the Birth of the Nation* (New York: Oxford University Press, 2018), 250.
31 Erica Armstrong Dunbar, *Never Caught: The Washingtons' Relentless Pursuit of Their Runaway Slave, Ona Judge* (New York: 37 Ink/Atria Books, 2017), xvi.

32 Dunbar, "Slave Catcher."
33 Dunbar, *Never Caught*, xvii.
34 Marvin Chun, "Edward Bouchet Portrait Revealed," *Yale Alumni Magazine*, January/February 2021, 58.
35 "With Highest Honor," *Yale Alumni Magazine*, January/February 2021, 64; Owen Tucker-Smith and Bryan Ventura, "Saybrook College to Display Portrait of Yale College's First Black Student Edward Bouchet," *Yale Daily News*, October 23, 2020, https://yaledailynews.com/blog/2020/10/23/saybrook-college-to-display-portrait-of-yale-colleges-first-black-student-edward-bouchet/.
36 Chun, "Bouchet."
37 Elizabeth Fitzsousa, Nientara Anderson, and Anna Reisman, "'This Institution Was Never Meant for Me': The Impact of Institutional Historical Portraiture on Medical Students," *Journal of General Internal Medicine* 34, no. 12 (December 2019): 2738, https://doi.org/10.1007/s11606-019-05138-9.
38 Brigid Katz, "Harvard Law School Marks Ties to Slavery in New Plaque," *Smithsonian Magazine*, September 6, 2017, https://www.smithsonianmag.com/smart-news/harvard-law-school-marks-ties-slavery-new-plaque-180964784/.
39 Ibid.
40 Lizzie Widdiecombe, "What Can We Learn from the Germans about Confronting Our History?" *New Yorker*, October 21, 2019, https://www.newyorker.com/culture/cultural-comment/what-can-we-learn-from-the-germans-about-confronting-our-history.
41 United States Holocaust Memorial Museum, Herero and Nama Genocide, August 11, 2020, https://www.ushmm.org/collections/bibliography/herero-and-nama-genocide.
42 Melissa Eddy, "For 60th Year, Germany Honors Duty to Pay Holocaust Victims," *New York Times*, November 17, 2012, https://www.nytimes.com/2012/11/18/world/europe/for-60th-year-germany-honors-duty-to-pay-holocaust-victims.html.
43 United States Holocaust Memorial Museum, "Herero and Nama Genocide."
44 Samira Shackle, "Roma Holocaust: Amid Rising Hate, 'forgotten' Victims Remembered," *Al Jazeera*, October 30, 2019, https://www.aljazeera.com/features/2019/10/30/roma-holocaust-amid-rising-hate-forgotten-victims-remembered/.
45 Ibid.
46 Liz Mineo, "Correcting 'Hamilton'," *The Harvard Gazette*, October 7, 2016, https://news.harvard.edu/gazette/story/2016/10/correcting-hamilton/.
47 Lilian S. Robinson, *Night Market: Sexual Cultures and the Thai Economic Miracle* (New York: Routledge, 1998), 113.
48 Gillian Brockell, "Here Are the Indigenous People Christopher Columbus and His Men Could Not Annihlate," *New York Times*, October 14, 2019, https://www.washingtonpost.com/history/2019/10/14/here-are-indigenous-people-christopher-columbus-his-men-could-not-annihilate/.
49 Megan Rose Dickey, "Facebook's Chief Diversity Officer Will Now Report Directly to Sheryl Sandberg," *TechCrunch*, June 11, 2020, https://techcrunch.com/2020/06/11/facebook-chief-diversity-officer-report-sheryl-sandberg-juneteenth/.
50 Rick Cohen, "Day of Service, or Day of Fighting Racial Injustice?" *NonProfit Quarterly*, January 21, 2014, https://nonprofitquarterly.org/day-of-service-or-day-of-fighting-racial-injustice/.
51 Lizzie Presser, "The Black American Amputation Epidemic," *ProPublica*, May 19, 2020, https://features.propublica.org/diabetes-amputations/black-american-amputation-epidemic/.

52. Samuel R. Gross, Maurice Possley, and Klara Stephens, *Race and Wrongful Convictions in the United States* (Irvine, CA: National Registry of Exonerations, 2017), http://www.law.umich.edu/special/exoneration/Documents/Race_and_Wrongful_Convictions.pdf.
53. "Universities Studying Slavery," President's Commission on Slavery and the University, University of Virginia, February 13, 2021, https://slavery.virginia.edu/universities-studying-slavery/.
54. Gather: Princeton Theological Seminary Magazine, "Princeton Theological Seminary Announces Plan to Repent for Ties to Slavery," October 18, 2019, https://gather.ptsem.edu/princeton-theological-seminary-announces-plan-to-repent-for-ties-to-slavery/.
55. The Associated Press, "Church; Justice and Reparations in Action," Memorial Episcopal Church, February 15, 2021, https://www.memorialboltonhill.org/the-memorial-reparations-fund. David Crary, "More US Churches Commit to Racism-Linked Reparations," *ABC News*, December 13, 2020, https://abcnews.go.com/US/wireStory/us-churches-commit-racism-linked-reparations-74701219.
56. "Social Justice and Reconciliation," Ministries, The Episcopal Diocese of Maryland, February 15, 2021, https://episcopalmaryland.org/social-justice-and-reconciliation/.
57. The Episcopal Diocese of New York, "The Diocesan Reparations Committee."
58. Eli Rosenberg, "German Billionaire Family That Owns Einstein Bros. Bagels Admits Nazi Past," *The Washington Post*, March 25, 2019, https://www.washingtonpost.com/history/2019/03/25/german-billionaire-family-that-owns-einstein-bros-bagels-admits-nazi-past/.
59. Ronni Michelle Greenwood, "Remembrance, Responsibility, and Reparations: The Use of Emotions in Talk about the 1921 Tulsa Race Riot," *Journal of Social Issues* 71, no. 2 (2015): 339, https://doi.org/10.1111/josi.12114.
60. Annalisa Merelli, "The Debt US Companies Owe Black Americans," *Quartz*, October 6, 2020, https://qz.com/1897852/what-reparations-mean-for-companies/.
61. Devin Dwyer, "Reparations for Slavery: Is Asheville a National Model?" *ABC News*, July 30, 2020, https://abcnews.go.com/Politics/reparations-slavery-asheville-national-model/story?id=72020930.
62. Merelli, "Black Americans."
63. "Foundation EVZ – The First Decade," Foundation Remembrance Responsibility Future, February 15, 2021, https://www.stiftung-evz.de/fileadmin/user_upload/EVZ_Uploads/Publikationen/Englisch/evz_10-jahre_engl-endfassung.pdf.
64. "About ICHEIC," The International Commission on Holocaust Era Insurance Claims, February 13, 2021, https://icheic.ushmm.org/about.html.
65. "Research, Restitution, and Remembrance: The Federal Government and Holocaust-Era Assets 1996–2001," National Archives, last modified April 20, 2001, https://www.archives.gov/research/holocaust/articles-and-papers/federal-government-and-holocaust-assets-1996–2001.html.
66. "About Us – Office of the Special Envoy for Holocaust Issues," U.S. Department of State, February 13, 2021, https://www.state.gov/about-us-office-of-the-special-envoy-for-holocaust-issues/; Michael J. Bazyler, "The Holocaust Restitution Movement in Comparative Perspective," *Berkeley Journal of International Law* 20, no. 1 (2003): 14, 16, https://doi.org/10.15779/Z38HS87.
67. Jacey Fortin, "Family Behind Krispy Kreme Donates Millions to Holocaust Survivors," *New York Times*, December 12, 2019, https://www.nytimes.com/2019/12/12/world/europe/reimann-family-holocaust.html.

68 Virginia Theological Seminary, "Virginia Theological Seminary Affirms Reparations Program," Virginia Theological Seminary, https://vts.edu/press-release/virginia-theological-seminary-affirms-reparations-program/.
69 Egan Millard, "Diocese of New York Establishes Reparations Fund, Adopts Anti-Slavery Resolutions from 1860," *Episcopal News Service*, November 12, 2019, https://www.episcopalnewsservice.org/2019/11/12/diocese-of-new-york-establishes-reparations-fund-adopts-anti-slavery-resolutions-from-1860/.
70 Ibid.
71 Virginia Theological Seminary, "Virginia Theological Seminary Affirms Reparations Program." Tracy Scott Forson, "Enslaved Labor Built These Universities. Now They Are Starting to Repay the Debt," *USA Today*, October 14, 2020, https://www.usatoday.com/story/news/education/2020/02/12/colleges-slavery-offering-atonement-reparations/2612821001/.
72 The Associated Press, "Church Established by Slave Owners Creates Reparations Fund," January 29, 2021, https://abcnews.go.com/US/wireStory/church-established-slave-owners-creates-reparations-fund-75573066.
73 Memorial Episcopal Church, "Memorial Episcopal Announces $100,000 Reparations Initiative," January 25, 2021, https://static1.squarespace.com/static/5a09a65b8c56a8aa90ea2eac/t/600f1da3ffe9ac7dfd7687c9/1611603363242/Memorial+Episcopal+Reparations.docx.pdf.
74 "Justice and Reparations in Action," Memorial Episcopal Church, February 15, 2021, https://www.memorialboltonhill.org/the-memorial-reparations-fund.
75 Crary, "More"; Jonathan M. Pitts, "Maryland Episcopal Diocese Commits $1 Million toward Reparations for Slavery, Racial Injustice," *Baltimore Sun*, September 15, 2020, https://www.baltimoresun.com/maryland/bs-md-episcopal-reparations-20200915-lijdlw6gtfd6jb2lmpl6axj35m-story.html.
76 Thadeus Greenson, "We're Coming Home," *North Coast Journal of Politics, People, & Art*, January 24, 2019, https://www.northcoastjournal.com/humboldt/were-coming-home/Content?oid=12849841.
77 Maanvi Singh, "Native American 'Land Taxes': A Step on the Roadmap for Reparations," *The Guardian*, December 31, 2019, https://www.theguardian.com/us-news/2019/dec/31/native-american-land-taxes-reparations.
78 Gather: Princeton Theological Seminary Magazine, "Princeton Theological Seminary Announces Plan to Repent for Ties to Slavery."
79 Virginia Theological Seminary, "Virginia Theological Seminary Affirms Reparations Program."
80 "Repentance and Reconciliation," Memorial Episcopal Church, February 15, 2021, https://www.memorialboltonhill.org/atonement-and-reconciliation; The Associated Press, "Church"; Memorial Episcopal Church, "Memorial Episcopal Announces $100,000 Reparations Initiative," January 25, 2021, https://static1.squarespace.com/static/5a09a65b8c56a8aa90ea2eac/t/600f1da3ffe9ac7dfd7687c9/1611603363242/Memorial+Episcopal+Reparations.docx.pdf; "What's in a Name," Memorial Episcopal Church, February 15, 2021, https://www.memorialboltonhill.org/whats-in-a-name.
81 "Annual Trail of Souls Event 2020," Maryland Episcopalian, https://marylandepiscopalian.org/2020/11/06/annual-trail-of-souls-event-2020/?utm_source=rss&utm_medium=rss&utm_campaign=annual-trail-of-souls-event-2020.
82 Millard, "Diocese."
83 The Episcopal Diocese of New York, "The Diocesan Reparations Committee"; "2018 Year of Lamentations: The Diocese Laments Its Role in Slavery," The Episcopal Diocese of New York, February 15, 2021, https://www.

dioceseny.org/ednyfiles/year-of-lamentations-brochure/?wpdmdl=39697&refresh=602882c7163821613267655.
84 Elizabeth Danquah-Brobby, "Prison for You. Profit for Me. Systemic Racism Effectively Bars Blacks from Participation in Newly-Legal Marijuana Industry," *University of Baltimore Law Review* 46, no. 3 (2017): 523–524, http://scholarworks.law.ubalt.edu/ublr/vol46/iss3/5.
85 Ibid., 525.
86 Iris Dorbian, "For U.S. Legal Pot Industry In 2021, Expect to See National Brands and $24 Billion in Sales, Says Top Researcher," *Forbes*, December 15, 2020, https://www.forbes.com/sites/irisdorbian/2020/12/15/for-us-legal-pot-industry-in-2021-expect-to-see-national-brands-and-24-billion-in-sales-says-top-researcher/?sh=1ed26540443e.
87 Patrick Williams, "America's Reckoning with Racism Is 'More Than a Moment,' Say Cannabis Industry Members," *Cannabis Business Times*, July 1, 2020, https://www.cannabisbusinesstimes.com/article/americas-reckoning-racism-more-than-a-moment-cannabis-industry-m4mm-mcba/.
88 "Aug. 8, 2018- Portland Cannabis Grants Awarded," *Community & Civic Life*, The City of Portland Oregon, January 25, 2021, https://www.portlandoregon.gov/civic/article/693562.
89 Mary Szto, "Real Estate Agents as Agents of Social Change: Redlining, Reverse Redlining, and Greenlining," *Seattle Journal for Social Justice* 12, no. 1 (2013): 56–57, https://digitalcommons.law.seattleu.edu/sjsj/vol12/iss1/2.
90 Ibid.
91 Ibid., 59.
92 See Ikechi Mgbeoji, *Global Biopiracy: Patents, Plants, and Indigenous Knowledge* (Ithaca, NY: Cornell University Press, 2006).
93 Keith Aoki, "Neocolonialism, Anticommons Property, and Biopiracy in the (Not-so-Brave) New World Order of International Intellectual Property Protection," *Indiana Journal of Global Legal Studies* 6, no. 1 (Fall 1998): 49–50, https://www.repository.law.indiana.edu/ijgls/vol6/iss1/2.
94 Rebecca Ellis, "Portland Took These Black Families' Homes. Some of Their Descendants Want Reparations," *OPB*, December 16, 2020, https://www.opb.org/article/2020/12/16/portland-oregon-affordable-housing-reparations/; Alana Semeuls, "The Racist History of Portland, the Whitest City in America," *The Atlantic*, July 22, 2016, https://www.theatlantic.com/business/archive/2016/07/racist-history-portland/492035/.
95 Ellis, "Portland."
96 Rodney A. Brooks, "More Than Half of Black-Owned Businesses May Not Survive COVID-19," *National Geographic*, July 17, 2020, https://www.nationalgeographic.com/history/2020/07/black-owned-businesses-may-not-survive-covid-19/.
97 Robin Saks Frankel, "Discover to Give $5 Million to Black-Owned Restaurants," *Forbes*, July 10, 2020, https://www.forbes.com/advisor/credit-cards/discover-to-give-5-million-to-black-owned-restaurants/.
98 Courtney Connley, "9 Financial Resources for Women and Minority Business Owners Affected by the Coronavirus," *CNBC: Make It*, May 19, 2020, https://www.cnbc.com/2020/05/19/financial-resources-for-women-and-minority-business-owners-affected-by-covid-19.html.
99 Robert Lee and Tristan Ahtone, "Land-Grab Universities," *High Country News*, March 30, 2020, https://www.hcn.org/issues/52.4/indigenous-affairs-education-land-grab-universities.

Chapter 5

Making powerful change when you lack political, institutional, or... any power

For years, African American Harvard Law School professor Charles Ogletree ran what he called "Saturday School." Aimed at African American students but open to their peers of all backgrounds, Saturday School was a program meant to offer haven to – and intensive investment in – its scholars. At Saturday School, Ogletree led review sessions, taught techniques for acing law school exams, and employed creative pedagogical methods such as having students act out arguing cases. He invited participants to watch how faculty members developed their ideas and to sharpen their own thinking by participating in discussions on legal history, contemporary politics, and the future of the Civil Rights movement. Saturday School students got to listen to – and then network with – acclaimed individuals in law and other fields, often about issues of racial justice missing from the Harvard Law curriculum.[1]

Commonly referenced in relation to its arguably most famous "graduate," former president Barack Obama,[2] Saturday School would come to be considered one of the jewels of Harvard University. One might expect such a venerable program to have been created from on high by someone with a supreme leadership role. But Ogletree wasn't the President of Harvard University. He wasn't even the Dean of Harvard Law – however, he didn't need to be in order to transform it. Whether or not you *run* an organization or community does not determine whether or not you can *change* it. Thus, at a university that has too often been hostile to non-whites,[3] Ogletree fashioned a juggernaut for the success of diverse students. He was able to do so because he understood something crucial: that though some power is *conferred*, other power is *created*. It is created from resources such as time, expertise, and connections.

You (regardless of whether you are a person of color or not) can create Saturday School – or Tuesday Evening, Every First Wednesday Lunch Break, or Friday Crack of Dawn School – in your own organization or community, and, if you wish, even open it to individuals from outside your organization or community. And you can do it by yourself, you can do it with just one other likeminded person – including someone from a different institution, or you can do it in a group. A Saturday School might consist of scientists from two or three laboratories in town coming together to offer professional development

DOI: 10.4324/9781003144298-6

to up-and-comers at their companies or a museum director inviting junior people in the field from institutions from across the city to partake in the program she's established primarily to serve those in her own workplace. The beauty of a Saturday School is you don't need anyone else's buy in to found one. That said, having multiple "faculty members" can lighten the responsibility – after all, if you find just three other people who share your vision, you can turn what's a weekly program for participants into a once-a-month commitment for the teachers. Furthermore, because Saturday Schools convert individuals' capabilities into capital to be invested in racial groups to whom power has been denied, having different people with different skills on the faculty allows you to diversify that investment portfolio.

Ogletree's Saturday School was antiracist in two ways. First, it created a resource-rich environment for diverse people to engage in capacity building and to excel *within* their institution – it was a site of what we might term "internal antiracism." Second, it equipped its students to fight for racial justice *beyond* their institution on behalf of those *outside* their institution. We can call that practicing "external antiracism." So, internal antiracism is developing infrastructure to help African American students succeed at your law school. External antiracism is developing infrastructure to train students to fight for the civil rights of the masses. Internal antiracism is having a plan to achieve racial parity at all levels of employment at your bank. External antiracism is having a plan to prevent people of color from being denied loans based on their race *by* your bank.[4]

Here are ways your Saturday School can be part of the machinery of internal systemic antiracism, depending on the strengths of your faculty: If you're a master of your craft, hold sessions on skill building – from coaching participants on their oral argument delivery to sharing the tricks on teaching of trigonometry to giving extra guidance on performing tricky arias. If the knack to your success is having figured out riddles like ascending the corporate ladder while parenting, time management, or networking for introverts, then teach those things. If you're one of those people who accrues relationship capital, invite guest speakers to address your participants – people like the mentor who gave you your best ever career advice, a former patient with whom you're on friendly terms who can explain what kind of bedside manner is most supportive for someone dealing with malignant illness, a luminary who can give concrete advice on what it takes to be great, or some of your superiors who are willing to detail and demystify their processes and trajectories. If you're socially connected, use sessions as networking events that get investment bankers into the room with potential clients or grant ballerinas access to possible sponsors. If you're savvy – if you know how to ask for opportunities or investment or raises or stock options – then teach that. You can have question-and-answer sessions in which people make the inquiries they're afraid to anywhere else. And you can teach the stuff that participants *aren't* getting anywhere else such as the unwritten rules of success at a particular organization, as described in Chapter 3.

Remember, as I discussed in Chapter 3, antiracist resources often directly benefit white people, too. What makes the practices described in the above paragraph antiracist is not that they only aid people of color or even that they're necessarily only offered to people of color – it's that they ensure people of color access to assets such as knowledge and networks from which they are often excluded for racialized reasons, including those discussed in that chapter, such as affinity bias in mentoring, the wealth gap, or the disproportionate likelihood of being a first generational professional whose loved ones are unable to impart crucial savvy.

In terms of *external* antiracism, your Saturday School can be a place where the efforts described in Chapter 4 can be exerted independent of institutional support. For example, in that chapter, I discussed steps that legal scholar Mary Szto urged the real estate industry to take to become a force for antiracism, things such as "[d]evelop[ing] training materials that describe the history of the realty industry in redlining and reverse red lining" and "[c]onduct[ing] intensive training on methods to avoid steering and other present day discriminatory practices."[5] But, maybe, for whatever reason, the real estate firm where you work is not going to undertake those endeavors. What doesn't get taught about racial justice on Monday to Friday is prime curricular material for Saturday. Your Saturday School could assign reading on redlining and reverse redlining. And you could research best practices for avoiding racial steering and for combatting one's implicit and explicit bias, and share them with students.

But what if you want to create antiracist infrastructure, but you're not far enough in your trajectory to be the headmaster of a Saturday School? What if you're more like a middle schooler – or even a kindergartener?

Remember, even people standing side by side at the beginnings of their journeys aren't necessarily similarly situated – commonly, only some of them have been furnished with maps. If you're a mapholder, then, even if you haven't reached your destination yet, you still may be equipped to serve as a guide.

For example, when I arrived at Dartmouth College as a Freshman, I learned that Native American and African American students had a practice of holding "office hours" in their dorm rooms to offer academic support to their indigenous and Black classmates. The students recognized that many of their peers, though brilliant, accomplished, and hardworking, had attended poor schools that simply didn't teach the material or skills that elite colleges expected incoming students to have mastered.[6] So, on cultural affinity group listservs, students offered support in their academic specialties, sending out emails such as "I'll be in my dorm room, Room X, in X building from 6:00 to 8:00 pm this Wednesday. Come by if you'd like help preparing for the Physics I exam." When I began offering academic assistance my Freshman fall, I was far from being in a position to say, "I know how to help you succeed in college because I've done it." But having attended a private, college preparatory school, I *was* able to say, "I know how to help you succeed in college because I was taught to do so – let me share what I learned."

You don't have to have seniority to have expertise. Consider holding "office hours" to offer support in the domain in which you excel. And ask others to join you in the practice. More generally, note that the practices described in this chapter – and throughout the book – can be adapted to each other's contexts, so, for example, actions mentioned in another chapter, like developing cultural competency, can be taught in Saturday School or material I describe as a potential part of a Saturday School curriculum can be taught in office hours.

Another thing you can do for your organization or community is draft briefs. I'm not referring to legal briefs – more like something akin to the policy briefs that subject matter experts write to break down complex issues for politicians. When I was at Yale Law, I drafted briefs for undergraduates on making a successful start to college, picking a major, and studying abroad that I'd leave in the campus cultural affinity houses or provide to the affiliated deans or give to professors who did lots of outreach with students of color for them to distribute. You see, because, in the United States, Hispanics, Native Americans, and Blacks are significantly less likely to have bachelor's degrees than whites (18.7, 14.5, and 26.1 percent, respectively, compared to 40.1 percent),[7] students from those cultures are far more likely than their white peers to represent the first generation of their family to go to college – to have parents with a limited ability to help them navigate higher education. I wrote the briefs to try to remedy that racialized information asymmetry.

Toni Morrison said, "If there's a book you really want to read, but it hasn't been written yet, then you must write it."[8] In the same vein, if there's a resource you really wish people in your organization or community could read, but it hasn't been written yet, then you must write it – and disseminate it. A human resources, communications, or diversity professional at your organization may help you make your brief(s) available, for example, by hosting them on the organization's intranet, but if it doesn't, briefs can be distributed to cultural affinity groups or simply passed on to those you feel might be interested. Outside the organizational context, make briefs available at the places patronized by your audience such as houses of worship, schools, community centers, beloved neighborhood businesses, library branches, etc. As with running a Saturday School, know that you *can* undertake this effort alone, but don't feel that you *must*. Put together materials sharing your specialist knowledge and invite likeminded people to do the same. If those people are parts of other organizations or communities, you can share the resources you develop amongst institutions.

Mentorship and sponsorship are two of most important resources people of color need to reach the top. Mentors guide; sponsors position – extending opportunities, advocating on the beneficiary's behalf, connecting the beneficiary to the right people, seeing to it that beneficiaries get the promotions and raises they've earned, etc. In Chapter 3, I outlined plans for how organizations and communities could institute antiracist mentoring programs. But even if your organization or community does not take steps to ensure mentoring happens free from bias, *you* can – to incredible effect. One mentor can impact multitudes – law professor Robin A. Lenhardt, writing about Ogletree, her own mentor and sponsor, says, "Black lawyers counting themselves among Professor Ogletree's many mentees can be found in virtually every area of the law – e.g., academia, criminal defense and prosecution, legal aid, and private practice."[9] Now, imagine the effect if one person invested in antiracist mentoring and sponsorship invites even a few likeminded individuals – at his or her own institution or another – to join the effort.

Here's what those seeking to engage in antiracist mentoring and sponsoring without institutional support should do:

Write down the names of the individuals you currently mentor or sponsor or did in the past. What races are or were they? If they were disproportionately white, consider whether there are individuals of color to whom you could be of service. Continue to monitor the races of whom you mentor and sponsor going forward, and make sure to reach out to high-potential people of color. And don't forget to participate in recruitment, hiring, admissions, and other entrance processes to the extent you're able in order to help make them equitable so that there *are* people of color around to mentor and sponsor!

Here, you might be wondering if it's racist if you're non-white and you tend to make a special effort to cultivate people of your own background. The answer is "no." When people with racial privilege confer benefits disproportionately upon people of their own race, they *perpetuate* racial injustice. To be clear, it isn't wrong for a white person to help another white person, but when a white person extends help in an intentionally discriminatory manner – or an inadvertently exclusive one – and this occurs in an institutional context, such behavior helps *some* and *disenfranchises* others. When people without (or with) racial privilege dedicate their efforts to helping others without racial privilege, they *combat* racial injustice. That said, because it is normal for people of color to be underrepresented in organizations and communities, it serves non-whites as a whole – and the cause of racial justice in general – for non-whites to support non-whites from other races. And in a situation in which there are no green people with senior roles, it's particularly beneficial for an orange person so situated to make special effort to ensure that the high-potential junior green person gets the support he or she needs. Similarly, in arenas in which women are underrepresented, some women prefer to mentor or sponsor women. However, because of how race and gender *intersect*, men of color are often underrepresented, too. In an environment in which men of color with seniority who can act as mentors or sponsors are scarce, an exclusionary focus on buoying women can leave non-white men without backers.

Once you've decided to engage in antiracist mentoring and sponsorship then, as described in Chapter 3, make a list of different types of support and check off those that you gave each mentee or sponsorship beneficiary. Doing so on a weekly basis allows you to hold yourself accountable in real time and over the long term for giving all your protégés the sort of support too often reserved for whites.

Now, let's talk about cultural affinity or employee resource groups. Every antiracist leader needs to know how to start one, if it doesn't exist, or how to make one work to the maximum, if it does. If your organization doesn't already have cultural affinity groups – or doesn't have one for *your* culture – consider founding one. Cultural affinity groups can be either unofficial or formally affiliated with an organization.[10] As Rebekah Bastian explains in *Forbes*, "Formal support can result in permanent ERG program budgets to spend on programming for their members, support for employees to use work hours on group activities, and open communication channels for them to influence business decisions."[11] The latter allows affinity group members to raise their profiles by interfacing with the highest levels of official organizational leadership. But while formal support certainly has its perks, it's by no means a prerequisite.

Cultural affinity groups can aim at serving people of a particular culture or race or people of color in general, but they should also make space for allies. They may support those in a certain role – such as the South Asian accountants at an accounting firm – or open themselves, at least at times, to other stakeholders – for example, to the accounting firm's South Asian support staff. What ultimately determines the scope of whom a cultural affinity group is for is the common interest of the participants. But don't forget that separate affinity groups can also join forces to share resources or to achieve a common goal. And they can advocate for non-members such as non-professional staff.

I have participated in or led cultural affinity groups at Dartmouth College, Harvard University, Yale University, and my law firm, and when they are at their best, they have a game-changing impact on the recruitment, retention, and ascension of people of color, turbo charging the trajectories of their members. They facilitate diverse forms of mentoring from one-on-one, to group, to cross-office, to cross-institution, combatting the effects of affinity bias in the larger organization. And those mentors offer counsel not just on mainstream professional development topics but demographic-specific issues such as navigating others' stereotypes, handling incidents of racism that occur at one's organization or in the course of one's practice, and leveraging one's cultural competence to enter new markets. Beyond mentorship, they offer a venue in which junior people can find sponsorship. And they provide a forum through which individuals, who might otherwise not have met, can connect, expanding the members' networks, familiarizing them with each other's strengths, and putting junior people on the radar of those more senior. Senior people from outside the group can also be invited to select sessions, such as social events, for these purposes.

Cultural affinity groups diversify their organizations by using their insider knowledge to innovate ways to recruit for population parity and then maintain that diversity by providing a space for people to bond – or vent and then strategize, extending support that gives members the fortitude to stay in and transform an institution – or even a profession or arena – where they may deal with isolation or hostility. The groups create a resource-rich environment in which to thrive by keeping each other apprised of – and backing each other for – opportunities such as diversity or cultural affinity professional development programs, events, associations, and conferences. And they *create* resources such as learning materials or programming. These may be offered to the larger organization or beyond it both as a service and as a profile-raising measure. Engaging in external antiracist practice, cultural affinity groups influence their organizations to leverage their resources, both fiscal and not, in the fight for racial justice. And, finally, they serve as innovation laboratories, sharing their most effective initiatives with other affinity groups and with the organization at large.

All those endeavors have the same effect as adding fertilizer, soil vitamins, and organic matter to the dirt surrounding a rosebush – they cause both the members of the cultural affinity group *and* the larger organization or community to flourish. Don't worry if the group you start or the one to which you contribute isn't able to do all the foregoing. Each positive input into the group's members can make a substantial impact on their trajectories and, as they compound, the effects become exponential.

Starting a cultural affinity group is simple. If you're seeking institutional affiliation, draft a pitch and budget proposal to present to human resources, your organization's diversity officer, or to a leader who might be willing to act as an executive sponsor and ally.[12] When you're ready to invite membership, ask if you can send out an organization-wide missive in the institution's newsletter or on its intranet introducing the group,[13] explaining the initiatives you envision it will undertake, and linking to a poll to determine a convenient time for the first meeting. If institutional platforms are not available to you, make personal invitations. At the first meeting, come up with a leadership structure and plan for how often the group will meet.

Once an affinity group is extant – whether by your efforts or not – proactively set up the structures you seek. For example, suggest the idea of a group mentoring program at a meeting. If there's interest, you could invite the senior members to contact you if they're willing to mentor, set up a meeting in which each presents on his or her mentorship style, and then have the junior members contact you with their ranked choices. Assign a group of mentees to each mentor, propose that everyone meet on a monthly basis with the option of scheduling one-on-one mentor-to-mentee conversations as desired, and then leave it to each group to take it from there. One general thing to remember as you get up and running is that though cultural affinity groups should obviously respect the norms of the culture in question, to get the most benefit, to the extent possible, foster an environment of egalitarianism, candor, confidentiality, and trust in which members can speak frankly with each other with the expectation that their remarks won't be shared beyond the group.

Throughout this book, I've spoken a lot about systems, holding that because racism is systemic, antiracism must be, too. Antiracists need to practice systems thinking. At its most basic, as Bryan Collins writes in *Forbes*, "Systems thinking means reflecting on how the parts within a larger whole work together."[14] But systems thinking has many components.

For example, understanding feedback loops is an element of systems thinking.[15] Say an antiracist creates a Saturday School to support the retention and ascension of people of color currently at her organization. The existence of that Saturday School may become a recruitment feature for people of color.[16] More non-whites entering the organization means the pool of people of color who may stay and rise is larger, and the increasing number and rising stature of non-whites attracts more diverse candidates and so on in a virtuous cycle.

Identifying interconnections is another part of systems thinking.[17] Thus, not only might the creation of a Saturday School engender the positive feedback loop described above, its effects are also connected to other parts of the system. So, for example, individuals who participate in Saturday School may rise in the organization to become diverse mentors and sponsors, including to people who don't participate in Saturday School. An increased number of diverse mentors and sponsors triggers its own feedback loop through the development of diverse talent that rises to become the next generation of diverse mentors and sponsors.

Stocks, flows, and variables are also fundamentals of systems thinking. Stocks are resources tangible and intangible, flows are changes in their amounts, and variables are alterable parts of systems that affect the former two.[18] For example, in investment or law firms, employees' books of business would be stocks. How organizations teach employees to develop those books of business would be a variable. As discussed in Chapter 3, a teaching such as "talk about what you do at cocktail parties" can be of little – or even laughable – utility to employees of color who, because of the racial wealth gap, may attend cocktail parties in communities where fellow guests don't have multimillion dollar investment capital or legal problems. But a Saturday School session, cultural affinity group meeting, or brief can offer strategies for business development for diverse populations.

Thus, those initiatives change the variable of how employees learn to develop business. That changed variable triggers a flow in a stock – expansion of non-white employees' books of business. The expanded books of business of diverse employees allow them to rise in the organization, a factor which is interconnected to other parts of the system such as the organization's ability to attract talent of color. The ability to attract talent of color sets off the aforementioned feedback loop in which the increasing number of non-whites attracted to the organization leads to an increase in those who reach prominent positions. The ascension of non-whites, fueled by their books of business, can also trigger another flow in a different stock – an increase in mentors and sponsors of color, which sets off that previously mentioned mentorship/sponsorship feedback loop.

These interconnections reveal another element of systems thinking: an appreciation for nonlinearity.[19] For example, while, in linear fashion, changing the variable of how business development is taught can affect the amount of business non-whites develop, in nonlinear fashion, it also affects the ability to recruit diverse talent.

Systems thinking also includes the practice of "systems mapping" – visually illustrating how the parts of a system relate to each other, so you can literally see the effect of changing a part on the whole.[20] Systems maps are really treasure maps, because they mark the spots where intervention is most effective. Antiracists who use systems thinking are able to act strategically, animated by the knowledge that tinkering even with one thing – if it's the right thing – can change everything.

That's why you don't need institutional support to make institutional change. And it's why you don't need power to strike a powerful blow for racial justice.

Notes

1 David Remnick, *The Bridge: The Life and Rise of Barack Obama* (New York: Vintage Books, 2010), 191; Robin A. Lenhardt, "Grave Building: A Tribute to Charles J. Ogletree, Jr., and His Evolving Legacy," *Harvard BlackLetter Law Journal* 22, no. 153 (2006): 157–158, https://ir.lawnet.fordham.edu/faculty_scholarship/456; F. Erik Brooks and MaCherie M. Placide, *Barack Obama: A Life in American History* (Santa Barbara, CA: ABC_CLIO, LLC, 2019), 32.
2 Remnick, *Bridge*, 191.
3 Lendhardt, "Grave Building," 157.
4 Emmanuel Martinez and Aaron Glantz, *How Reveal Identified Lending Disparities in Federal Mortgage Data* (Emeryville, CA: Reveal from the Center for Investigative Reporting, 2018), https://s3-us-west-2.amazonaws.com/revealnews.org/uploads/lending_disparities_whitepaper_180214.pdf.
5 Mary Szto, "Real Estate Agents as Agents of Social Change: Redlining, Reverse Redlining, and Greenlining," *Seattle Journal for Social Justice* 12, no. 1 (2013): 55, https://digitalcommons.law.seattleu.edu/sjsj/vol12/iss1/2.
6 Sophie Quinton and National Journal, "The Race Gap in High School Honors Classes," *The Atlantic*, December 11, 2014, https://www.theatlantic.com/politics/archive/2014/12/the-race-gap-in-high-school-honors-classes/431751/.
7 "U.S. Census Bureau Releases New Educational Attainment Data," United States Census Bureau, last modified March 30, 2020, https://www.census.gov/newsroom/press-releases/2020/educational-attainment.html; Frank Vaisvilas, "Higher Education Rates for Native Americans Remain Low, But Unique Scholarships Are Helping," *Green Bay Press Gazette*, February 2, 2021, https://www.greenbaypressgazette.com/story/news/2021/02/02/higher-education-rates-native-americans-low-scholarships-helping/4313835001/.

8 Corinne J. Naden and Rose Blue, *Toni Morrison* (Chicago, IL: Raintree, 2006), 6.
9 Lenhardt, "Grave Building," 157.
10 Sheree Atcheson, "5 Top Tips on Creating Successful Employee Resource Groups," *Forbes*, February 17, 2021, https://www.forbes.com/sites/shereeatcheson/2021/02/17/5-top-tips-on-creating-successful-employee-resource-groups/?sh=5da3abe025b7; Janice Gassam Asare, "How to Start an Employee Resource Group at Your Organization," *Forbes*, October 22, 2018, https://www.forbes.com/sites/janicegassam/2018/10/22/how-to-start-an-employee-resource-group-at-your-organization/?sh=4143daeb1756.
11 Rebekah Bastian, "How to Foster Workplace Belonging through Successful Employee Resource Groups," *Forbes*, February 11, 2019, https://www.forbes.com/sites/rebekahbastian/2019/02/11/how-to-foster-workplace-belonging-through-successful-employee-resource-groups/?sh=2aa3f908dc73.
12 Ibid.
13 Asare, "Start."
14 Bryan Collins, "How to Sharpen Your Leadership Skills and Grow Your Business," *Forbes*, July 16, 2019, https://www.forbes.com/sites/bryancollinseurope/2019/07/16/how-to-sharpen-your-leadership-skills-and-grow-your-business/?sh=a4931425b791.
15 Ross D. Arnold and Jon P. Wade, "A Definition of Systems Thinking: A Systems Approach," *Procedia Computer Science* 44 (2015): 273, 672, 676, https://doi.org/10.1016/j.procs.2015.03.050.
16 Bruce S. Stuart and Kim D. Stuart, *Top Law Schools: The Ultimate Guide* (New York: Prentice Hall Press, 1990), 133.
17 Arnold and Wade, "Systems," 676.
18 Ibid., 677.
19 Ibid., 672.
20 Jonathan H. Westover "The Role of Systems Thinking in Organizational Change and Development," *Forbes*, June 15, 2020, https://www.forbes.com/sites/forbescoachescouncil/2020/06/15/the-role-of-systems-thinking-in-organizational-change-and-development/?sh=2cbde1c2c99d.

Epilogue – ancestors and avatars

Becoming what the future requires

This is a book for people of all racial backgrounds. It's also a book for people of any faith or no faith at all. But I'm going to reference religion in this Epilogue, to invoke the concept of the avatar, which antiracists may find a useful metaphor. In some religious traditions, the divine takes on human form for the stated purpose of pursuing justice. Jesus, in Chapter 4 of Luke, announces that He has come to end oppression. Similarly, the Hindu god Vishnu poetically explains why he has taken on human form in the holy book *Bhagavad Gita*:

> Whenever righteousness falters and chaos threatens to prevail, I take on a human body and manifest myself on earth. In order to protect the good, to destroy the doers of evil, to ensure the triumph of righteousness, in every age I am born.[1]

Vishnu is, in fact, one of the trimurti, a triad of gods who each acts as custodian of the universe by expressing a different energy: Brahma creates. Vishnu preserves. Shiva destroys.

I evoke these religious figures not to proselytize but to probe: What would it mean for us, as antiracists, to regard ourselves as being in the world to end oppression and to ensure the triumph of righteousness? How would we act, what decisions would we make big and small on a daily basis, if we regarded – or recognized – protecting the good of racial justice and destroying the evil of its inverse as the very purpose of our beings? The faith traditions that hold that gods can become incarnated as ordinary people invite us to ponder, *What does it mean to literally* embody *the values we affirm – not just to champion values but, through our deeds, to* personify *them?*

The power to create, sustain, and destroy the universe does not belong to gods alone. When we offer an unpaid internship, we create an opportunity less accessible to races of people on the disenfranchised side of the wealth gap. When we fail to establish antiracist mentorship and sponsorship schemes at our organizations or to plan for how to ensure we, personally, support people of color, we sustain racism by allowing affinity bias to fester. When we

DOI: 10.4324/9781003144298-7

nix a proposal to atone for our organization's involvement with slavery or indigenous dispossession on the grounds that it would be too "divisive," we destroy a chance at doing justice. But when we create a recruitment initiative that solicits from minority-serving colleges and universities, cultural affinity groups, and diversity professional organizations or sustain our commitment to achieve population parity for people of color at every level of our organization despite media backlash that doing so is anti-white or when we terminate an employee who intentionally violates company policy by wearing Confederate flag clothing to work, we make our moral universe more righteous. As you go about your day, ask yourself: What is this particular action or inaction creating, sustaining, or destroying in regard to race: diversity, equity, inclusion, justice, or their inverses?

Such reflection is key to another component of being an antiracist: acting like an ancestor. When we think of ourselves only as the descendants of those who came before or the current denizens of the earth, the world we make for those who follow is but the byproduct of our activities. In contrast, when we act in the mode of ancestor of those to come, we are not only cognizant that we are inextricably involved in the process of shaping the world, but we also recognize the ability to world-craft as a privilege and adopt it as a priority. We go about our quotidian lives with gravity and intensity out of respect for our own power to create, sustain, and destroy the realities in which future generations of people of color will flourish or languish, live or die.

Living ancestors regard themselves with precocious retrospection. They look down at the afternoon's events in their planners as though looking *back* from the perspective of those generations into the future. They know that the 1:00 pm mentoring session with a person of color contributes to career ascendance which contributes to the creation of generational wealth or that the 3:00 pm meeting with human resources about the security guards' habit of challenging non-whites' presence in the building contributes to lowering the stress caused by racism and the physiological "weathering" caused by that stress. They know that getting rid of that stressor gives a child of color that much more of a chance at having her grandparent live long enough to meet her.[2] They reflect on their daily schedules from the perspective of the child who'll get to make memories with her grandparent, of the great-grandchild helped by the wealth his forebear created to attend college. When they go to bed at night, living ancestors don't just ask themselves, *Was today productive?* They ask, *Was tomorrow impacted?*

A living ancestor may occasionally fantasize that "if I were around back then, I would have been a conductor on the Underground Railroad" or "marched with Civil Rights activists," but mostly ancestors focus on the fact that they are around *now*. They recognize that their own era is one about which future generations will make assertions as to what they would have done. And they make certain the acts that will be part of those future generations' hagiographic hypotheticals become episodes of their personal histories.

Unconscious bias and systemic racism aside, a critical mass of bigots, both humble and great, have always understood their power to create and sustain what they value, to destroy what they do not, and have not just articulated their beliefs but embodied them. They redlined. They profile.[3] They poison entire communities.[4]

And one of them placed the weight of his body, and of history, atop his fellow man's neck and knelt there until he killed him.

We, as antiracists, both humble and great, must realize our own power and wield it tactically. If we do, we can end racism. *You* can end racism.

You can be – or become – what the future requires.

Notes

1 Stephen Mitchell, *Bhagavad Gita: A New Translation* (New York: Three Rivers Press, 2000), 73.
2 O. Kenrik Duru, Nina T. Harawa, Dulcie Kermah, and Keith C. Norris, "Allostatic Load Burden and Racial Disparities in Mortality," *Journal of the National Medical Association* 104, no. 1–2 (2012), https://doi.org/10.1016/s0027-9684(15)30120-6.
3 "Inside 100 Million Police Traffic Stops: New Evidence of Racial Bias: Stanford Researchers Found That Black and Latino Drivers Were Stopped More Often Than White Drivers, Based on Less Evidence of Wrongdoing," *NBC News*, last modified March 13, 2019, https://www.nbcnews.com/news/us-news/inside-100-million-police-traffic-stops-new-evidence-racial-bias-n980556.
4 Natalie Colarossi, "Briefing 10 Alarming Examples of Environmental Racism in the US," *Business Insider Australia*, August 12, 2020, https://www.businessinsider.com.au/environmental-racism-examples-united-states-2020-8.

Index

Note: Page numbers followed by "n" denote endnotes.

academic diversity 33
activism, antiracist 35
affinity bias 65
affinity groups, cultural 114–116
African American slavery 96
African Americans 34–38, 41–43, 59, 62–63, 66, 94, 97–98, 109–111; culture 36
age of racial terror (Stevenson) x
altruism 11
American Ballet Theatre 57–58
American Indians 92
American slavery 96
ancestors x, 119–121
Anderson, Maggie 73
Angel Tree tradition 56
anti-bias training 63
anti-Black bigotry 10
antiracism 1–2, 23–24, 30–50, 80, 93; effective ix–x, 17, 19, 38, 117; external 110–111; internal 110; internal systemic 110; movement 26
antiracist activism 35
antiracist conversations x, 8–10, 13–14, 15, 16, 30–35, 37
antiracist journey 1–4
antiracist strategies 5, 22–23, 51–53, 60, 84
antiracist systems 3, 6, 51–52, 99
antiracists 17–23, 30, 69, 80, 103, 114–117, 119–121; effective 38
anti-segregation laws 44
antisemitic violence 19
antisemitism 86
anti-sexual harassment movement 26
anti-white racism 40

apartheid 90
Arkansas public school system 18
Army, United States 60
Asian Americans 72, 80
Asians 4n8, 5, 22, 54, 66, 76n21
Association of Black Women Historians (ABWH) 57
Association for Enterprise Opportunity (AEO) 72
atonement 96
Auschwitz 79
Australia 89
avatars 119–121
awareness training 63

backlash x, 14, 120
Baldwin, Roger S. 91
Bastian, Rebekah 114
Batson challenge 61–62
Batson v. Kentucky (1986) 61
belief bias 45
beliefs, racist 8, 21, 46
Bhagavad Gita 119
bias: affinity 65; belief 45; cognitive 46; explicit 5; unconscious x, 68, 121
bigotry 2–3, 5, 10, 21–22, 26, 31; anti-Black 10
bigots 15, 121
biopiracy 101
BIPOC (Black Indigenous (and) People of Color) 72
Black Americans 19
Black community 10–11, 82
Black History Month 93
Black Law Students Association (Yale Law School) 56

Index

Black maternal mortality 19
Black people/Blacks 2–3, 4n8, 5–7, 8, 11, 25, 40, 44–47, 58–60, 63, 72, 80–81, 99, 112
Bloomberg 58
Bonilla-Silva, Eduardo 47
Boston University 45
Bouchet, Edward 89
Bradley, C. 57
Brahma 119
Brown v. Board (1954) 13
Butler, Paul 93

Canada 89, 95
changemakers 80–81
changemaking 79
Chauvin, Derek 1, 10–12, 25
Chavis, Benjamin 74
children: of color 39–40, 58; non-white 39; white 39
Christmas Carol, A (Dickens) 23
civil discourse 15
Civil Rights Movement 10, 109
Civil Rights protests 6
cognitive bias 46
cognitive distortion 45
Cohen, Rick 93
Collins, Bryan 116
colonialism 92–94
color: children of 39–40, 58; people of 24, 32–33, 41, 53–59, 64–66, 79, 89–91, 94–95, 114–116, 120; women of 55
colorblind person 19
colormum person 19–25
Columbia Law School 9
Columbus, Christopher 81, 85, 89, 93
Columbus Day 79, 85, 92–93
communication barriers, interracial 64
community 5–8, 51–60, 65–72, 81–84, 95–98, 103, 109, 112, 121; Black 10–11, 82; ethnic 40; Hmong American 10–11; Minneapolis Hmong 12; non-white 70
concentration camps 79, 86
Confederate flag 79–85, 120
Confederates 84
Connecticut Coalition for Justice in Education Funding 18
consequences, racial 71
conversations, antiracist x, 8–10, 13–14, 15, 16, 30–35, 37

Copeland, Misty 57
Cornerstone Speech (Stephens) 82
coronavirus pandemic 102
corporate culture 80
Coski, John 82
Crenshaw, Kimberlé Williams 43–44
crimes, drug 2–3
Crimes against Peace 87
cross-cultural training 63
cross-racial dialogue 3
cultural affinity groups 114–116
cultural competence training 63
cultural competency 63
cultural metacognition 63
culture 62; African American 36; corporate 80
cystic fibrosis 19

Darity, William 96
Dartmouth College 58, 111, 114
Davis, Jefferson 86, 92
de facto segregation 70
denazification, Germany 84
dialogues, tactics in x, 30–48
Diary of Anne Frank (Frank) 12, 90
dichotomy 7, 45
Dickens, Charles 23
discrimination 35, 80, 90, 95, 100; racial 35, 74
disparity, racial 35, 58, 69, 74, 94
diversity 32–33, 52–53, 58–60, 71–73, 80, 115, 120; academic 33; ideological 32; racial 32–33, 57; training 13–14, 54
Dobbin, Frank 58
Douglass, Erica Armstrong 87
drug crimes 2–3
Dweck, Carol 2

Eastman, Charles A. 45
Eckford, Elizabeth 18
effective antiracism ix–x, 17, 19, 38, 117
effective antiracists 38
egalitarianism 116
Ellis, Manuel 1
Emancipation Proclamation (1862) 43–44
empathy 38, 41–42
Enninful, Edward 6
enslavement 88
Episcopal Diocese of Maryland *see* Maryland Episcopal Diocese

Equal Employment Opportunity
    Commissioner 57
Equal Justice Initiative 92
equality 43
equity 52–53, 63, 71, 80, 120; racial 75
equity training 13–14, 54
Estée Lauder 59–60
ethnic community 40
Europe 95
explicit bias 5
explicit racism 5–29
external antiracism 110–111

Facebook 93; Juneteenth 93
Firm Diversity Council 80
fixed mindsets 1–2
Floyd, George ix, 1, 6, 10–12, 19,
    25–26, 44, 51–54, 80
Forbes 114–116
Foundation Remembrance,
    Responsibility, and Future 96
Frank, Anne 88
fraternity 64–66
free speech 17

Gandhi, Mahatma 18
Garcilaso de la Vega 85
Garner, Eric 1
Garrison, William Lloyd 22–23
Gates Jr., Henry Louis 5
gender 54
gender norms 36; white 36
genocide 10, 40–41, 86–90; Herero
    and Nama 90, 102; Native
    American 86
George III, King of England 85
German Americans 85
Germany 43, 90, 96; denazification 84
Gibson, Nell 80
greenlining 100
growth mindsets 1, 2

Hamilton, Alexander 92
Harvard University 58, 109, 114
Herero genocide 90, 102
heroes 48, 91; Holocaust rescuers xiii
High Country News 102
Hirsh, Elizabeth, and Tomaskovic-Devey,
    Donald 55, 60, 69, 73
Hispanic Americans 19
Hispanic Heritage Month 93
Hispanics 58, 72, 80, 112

Hitler, Adolf 40, 85–88, 93
Hmong American community
    10–11, 12
Ho Chi Minh 85
Holocaust 86, 90–91, 96
Holocaust rescuers xiii
House Committee on Financial
    Services 74
How the Irish Became White (Ignatiev) 94
Hughes, Langston 26

ideological diversity 32
Ignatiev, Noel 94
imperialism 101
inclusion 52–53, 59, 63, 71, 80, 120;
    training 13–14, 54
indigenous people 24, 81, 89, 93, 97
Indigenous Peoples' Day 93–94
inequality 43–44; racial 5
inequity 19
infant mortality 1, 32
injustice, racial 45, 70, 83, 95, 102, 113
injustices, racialized 34
insensitivity, racial 42
institutional racism 13, 19, 51, 100
intentional sidelining 68
internal antiracism 110
internal racism 94
internal systemic antiracism 110
International Commission on Holocaust
    Era Insurance Claims (ICHEIC) 96
internet 1, 20
interracial communication barriers 64
intra-racial racism 12
Islam 22
Israel 96
Italian Americans 85
#Itoo 26–27
Ivy League 58

JAB Holding Company 96
Jackson, Bernice Powell 80
Jefferson, Thomas 86–89
Jews 10, 86
Judge, Ona 88
Juneteenth 93

keystone change 80
King Jr., Martin Luther 17, 18, 23, 51, 58,
    93, 103
Klein, Philip 86–88
Kramer, Chuck 80

Latino Medical Student Associations 57
Latinos 5, 64, 72
laws, anti-segregation 44
Learning from the Germans (Neiman) 90
Lee, Fong 10
Lenhardt, Robin A. 113
Lewis, John 94
LGBT 80
Lies My Teacher Told Me (Loewen) 92
Lindstrom, Carole 94
Little Rock Nine 18
Loewen, James W. 92
Lösener, Bernhard 43, 86
Louisiana plantations 15
Luban, David 43

McClain, Elijah 1
McKinsey 52
marginalization 23
marginalized backgrounds 80
Martin Luther King Jr. Day 93
Maryland Episcopal Diocese 95, 97; Episcopal Churches of 95, 97, 98
maternal mortality, Black 19
media 24; news 20; social 16, 22, 71, 93
Memorial Episcopal Church of Maryland 95, 97, 98
metacognition, cultural 63
#metoo 26
Metropolitan Opera 74
Mindset: The New Psychology of Success (Dweck) 2
Minneapolis Hmong community 12
minorities, racial 73
Minorities 4 Medical Marijuana (M4MM) 99
minority 10; groups 54; populations 10; race 9, 54; racial 73; underrepresented 34
Minority Cannabis Business Association 99
Montgomery Bus Boycott 92
monuments 85
Morrill Act (1862), Indigenous Land Parcels Database 95
Morrison, Toni 112
mortality: infant 1, 32; maternal 19
Muslims 22, 65

Nadal, Kevin 21
Nama genocide 90, 102
Namibia 90

National Institutes of Health 19
Native American genocide 86
Native American Journalists Association (NAJA) 57
Native Americans 1, 5–6, 40–41, 58, 66, 71–72, 89–92, 102, 111–112; women 4n6
Nazis 10, 84–87, 90–91, 97
Nazism 10, 96
Negroes 58
Neiman, Susan 90
New Haven (Connecticut) 7; public school students 56
New Orleans 14, 17
New York 64; Wall Street 102
New York Diocese 98
news media 20
nineteenth century 91
non-whites 24, 33–34, 35–37, 43–46, 54–56, 59–60, 64–74, 86–88, 91–94, 116–117; children 39; community 70; race 35
norms, gender 36
Nuremberg trials 87

Obama, Barack 5, 109
Office of the Special Envoy for Holocaust Issues 96
Ogletree, Charles 5, 109–110, 113
Opportunity Agenda, The 24
Our Black Year (Anderson) 73

Pacific Islanders 80
Parent Teacher Association (PTA) 42
Parks, Rosa 18, 92
patriotism 82–83
Pennsylvania, Gradual Abolition Act (1780) 87
people of color 24, 32–33, 41, 53–59, 64–66, 79, 89–91, 94–95, 114–116, 120
Pipeline to Practice Foundation 55
plantations 79; Louisiana 15
police violence 44, 45
political correctness 12
Pollard, Edward A. 46–47
Porchon-Lynch, Täo 18
Portland (Oregon) 101–102
post-traumatic stress disorder (PTSD) 18
poverty 7
prejudice 3, 5, 19, 26–27, 47, 63; racial 27

Prep for Prep 57
Press, Steven 102
Princeton Theological Seminary 96–98
privilege: racial and/or economic 70; socio-economic 64; white 42
privileged person 9
profiling 6–8; racial 5
Project Plié 55
pro-slavery 22
protests: Civil Rights 6; George Floyd's death 6, 44
Psychological Bulletin 63
public school segregation 13
public sphere 17, 71

race 6–7, 10–11, 22–26, 34–36, 40–43, 47–48, 53–55, 65–73, 119–120; minority 9, 54; non-white 35
racial backgrounds 119
racial groups 72, 110
racism 1–3, 9–10, 19–27, 30–50, 91–93, 98–102, 119–121; explicit 5–29; institutional 13, 19, 51, 100; internal 94; intra-racial 12; systemic 51–78, 95, 99–100, 121; unconscious 89
racism-blind 19
redlining 100, 111
Romani people 10, 91
Rosner, Helen 62
Royal Commentaries of the Incas and General History of Peru, The (Garcilaso de la Vega) 85
Royall Jr., Isaac 89

safe spaces 40
Sánchez de Huelva, Alonso 85
Satell, Greg 79–81
Saturday School 109–112, 116
Save America Rally (2020) 84
Scott, Derek 1
segregation 43, 80, 95, 98; de facto 70; public school 13
Selma Online 92
Senate Banking Committee 96
sensitivity, racial 41–42
Shiva 119
sickle cell disease 19
sidelining, intentional 68
Silicon Valley 64
Sinti people 91
slave trader 92
slaveholders 86, 91

slavery 79–80, 83, 86–88, 90, 93–95, 98–99, 120; African American 96; American 96; pro- 22
slaves 40, 87–89, 96–97; narratives 12
SMART goals 13–14, 59–60, 74, 89
Smithsonian National Museum (Washington DC) 92
social justice 14
social media 16, 22, 71, 93
Social Security Act (1935) 70
Society of Architectural Historians (SAH) 84
socio-economic privilege 64
Sogorea Te' Land Trust 97
solidarity 10
solipsism 35–39, 62, 85
sorority 64–66
Spain 85
Stephens, Alexander H. 82
stereotypes 22
stereotyping, racial 54
Stevenson, Bryan x
Stockton, Betsey 98
stoicism 18
Students Associations 57
supremacists, white 18, 86–88, 92
supremacy, white 22, 33, 81–84
Supreme Court 13, 61
swastikas 79
systemic racism 51–78, 95, 99–100, 121
systems mapping 117
systems thinking 116, 117
Szto, Mary 99–100, 111

Tallchief, Maria 92
Teaching What Really Happened (Loewen) 92
terror, racial x, 90
terrorism 22
Thao, Tou 10
Third Reich 79
Tomaskovic-Devey, Donald, and Hirsh, Elizabeth 55, 60, 69, 73
Tomuschat, Christian 87
tone policing 9
training xiii, 13–14, 54, 63
trigger warnings 40
Trump, Donald 62, 81
Tulsa Race Massacre 95
twentieth century 90–92

unconscious bias x, 68, 121
unconscious racism 89

underrepresented minority 34
United States of America (USA) 10, 16, 24–25, 58–61, 73–74, 82–85, 95–96, 101, 112; Army 60; Equal Employment Opportunity Commissioner 57; Holocaust Memorial Museum 90; House Committee on Financial Services 74; Metropolitan Opera 74; National Institutes of Health 19; New Orleans 14, 17; New York 64, 102; Office of the Special Envoy for Holocaust Issues 96; Senate Banking Committee 96; Silicon Valley 64; Supreme Court 13, 61; Washington DC 64

Vang, Youa 10–12, 22
Vergangenheitsaufarbeitung 90–91, 98–99
Verizon 102
victimhood 31
victimized group 20
victim-mongering 31
views, racist 15
violence: against Native American women 4n6; antisemitic 19; police 44, 45
Virginia Theological Seminary 97–98
Vishnu 119

Wall Street 102

Ward, Laysha 72
Washington, George 40–41, 48, 86–91
Washington DC 64
Washington Post 23
We Are Water Protectors (Lindstrom) 94
wealth gaps, racial 70
Weeks, Holly 83
Wells, Jonathan Daniel 102
White, James D. 59
white Americans 19
white children 39; non- 39
white gender norms 36
white people 36–37, 40, 45–46, 63; non- 24, 35–37
white privilege 42
white supremacists 18, 86–88, 92
white supremacy 22, 33, 81–84
whiteness 27
whites 2, 44, 52–54, 59, 64–65, 68, 71, 74, 91, 99; non- 33–34, 43–46, 54–56, 59–60, 64–74, 86–88, 91–94, 116–117
Wild West 92
women of color 55
Wounded Knee massacre (1890) 45

Yale College 89n35
Yale Law School 7, 56, 112; Black Law Students Association 56; Capital Punishment Clinic 18
Yale University 58, 72, 114

For Product Safety Concerns and Information please contact our EU representative GPSR@taylorandfrancis.com
Taylor & Francis Verlag GmbH, Kaufingerstraße 24, 80331 München, Germany

www.ingramcontent.com/pod-product-compliance
Lightning Source LLC
Chambersburg PA
CBHW061719300426
44115CB00014B/2751